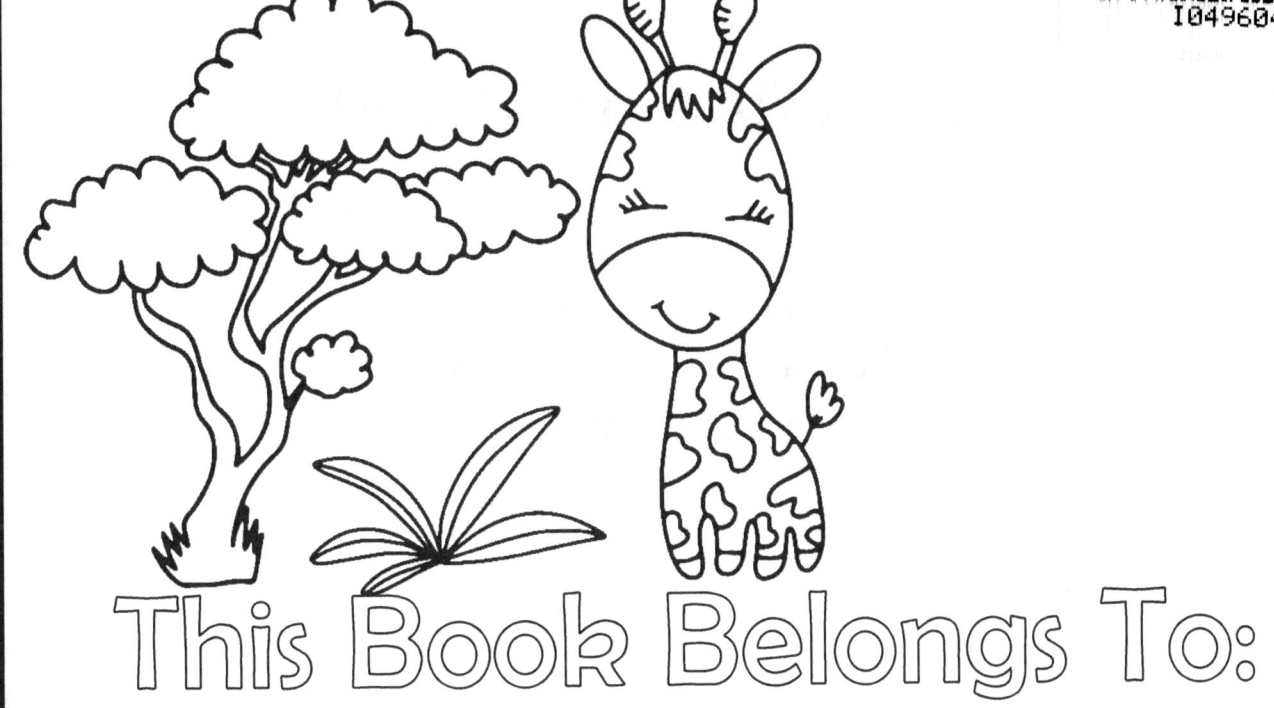

This Book Belongs To:

ooooooooooooooooooooooooooooooooooooooooooo

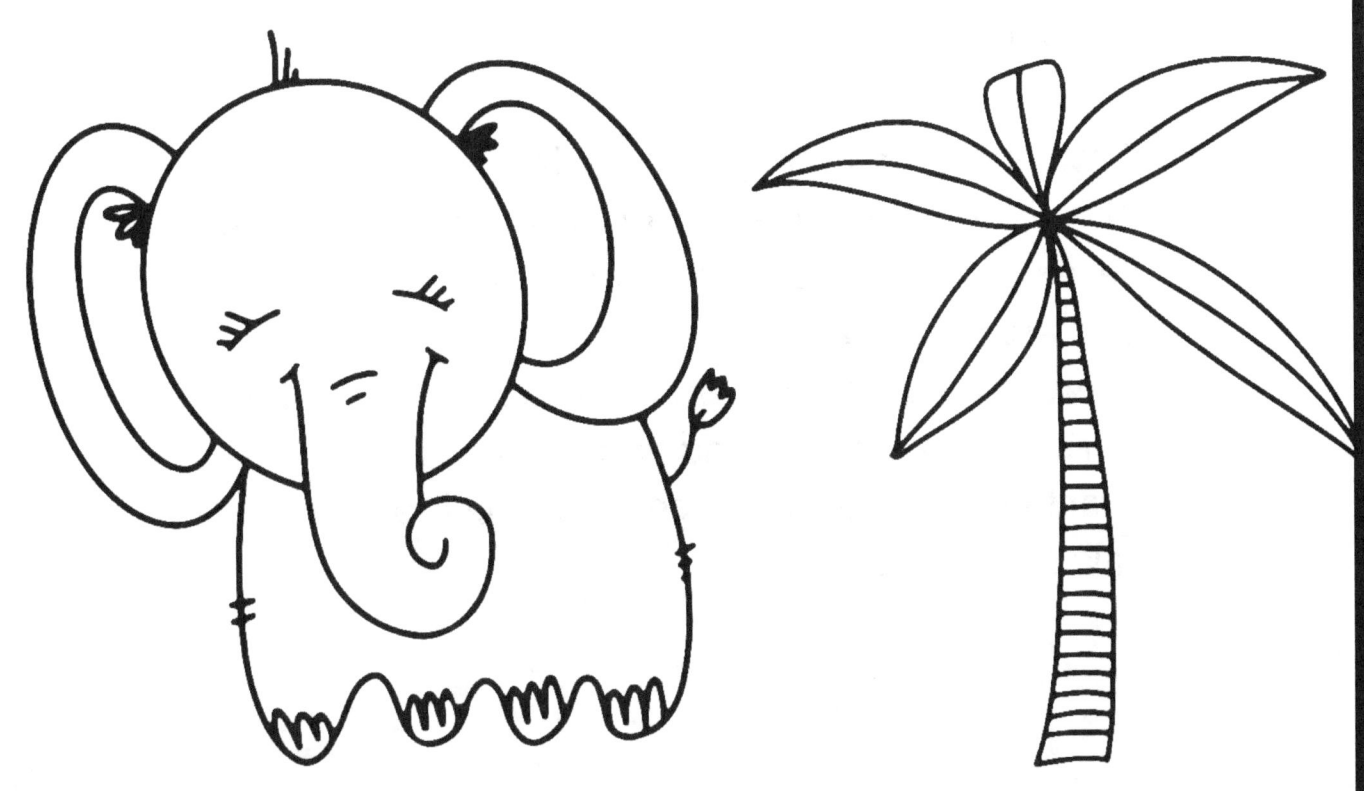

Let's learn to draw!

Learning to draw is easy with the grid copy method. The grid method has been used for centuries and is a wonderful way to work on your observation and proportion skills while drawing.

To get started, grab a pencil and eraser.

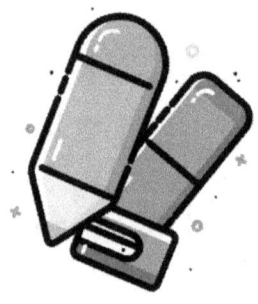

TIPS FOR DRAWING:

- Always start in pencil and use light strokes. You can always go back and erase or darken your strokes.
- Take your time. Slow down and really focus on what you are drawing.
- Sketch an outline first then go back and add detail, darken your strokes, and add color.
- Practice, practice, practice! Drawing is a skill that takes time to master!

The Grid Copy Method

The grid copy method breaks down each full image into smaller boxes allowing you to focus on and simply draw one box of the picture at a time. Start with grid box A1 and work your way down to box F7.

When you are drawing, focus only on what is in that particular box that you are working on. Try to draw exactly what you see in the box.

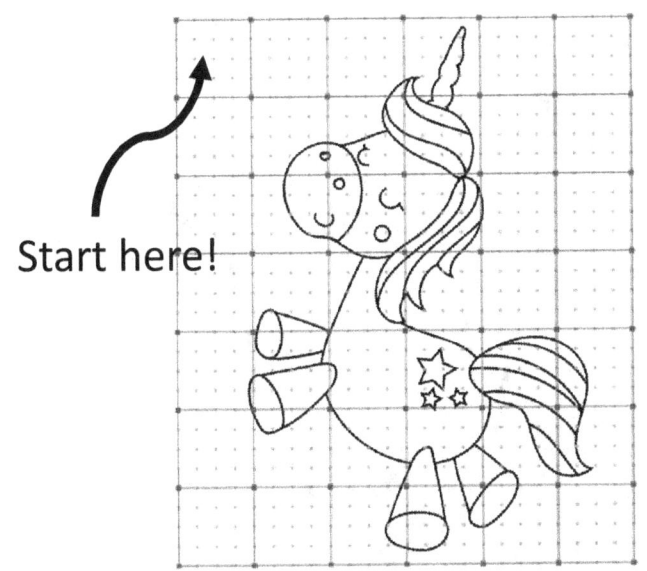

Start here!

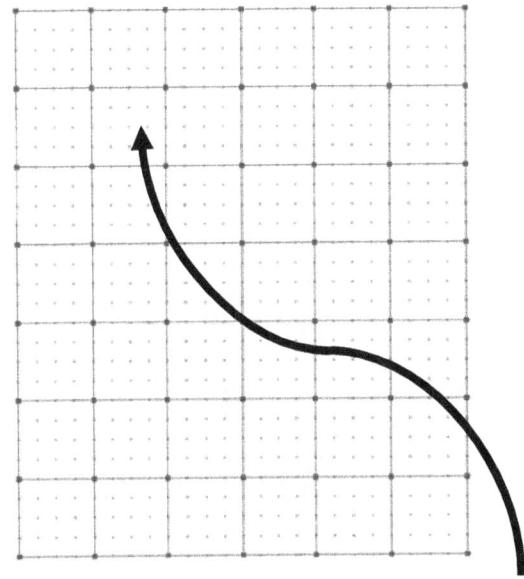

Focus on one box at a time

When you're finished, add your own details or color your masterpiece

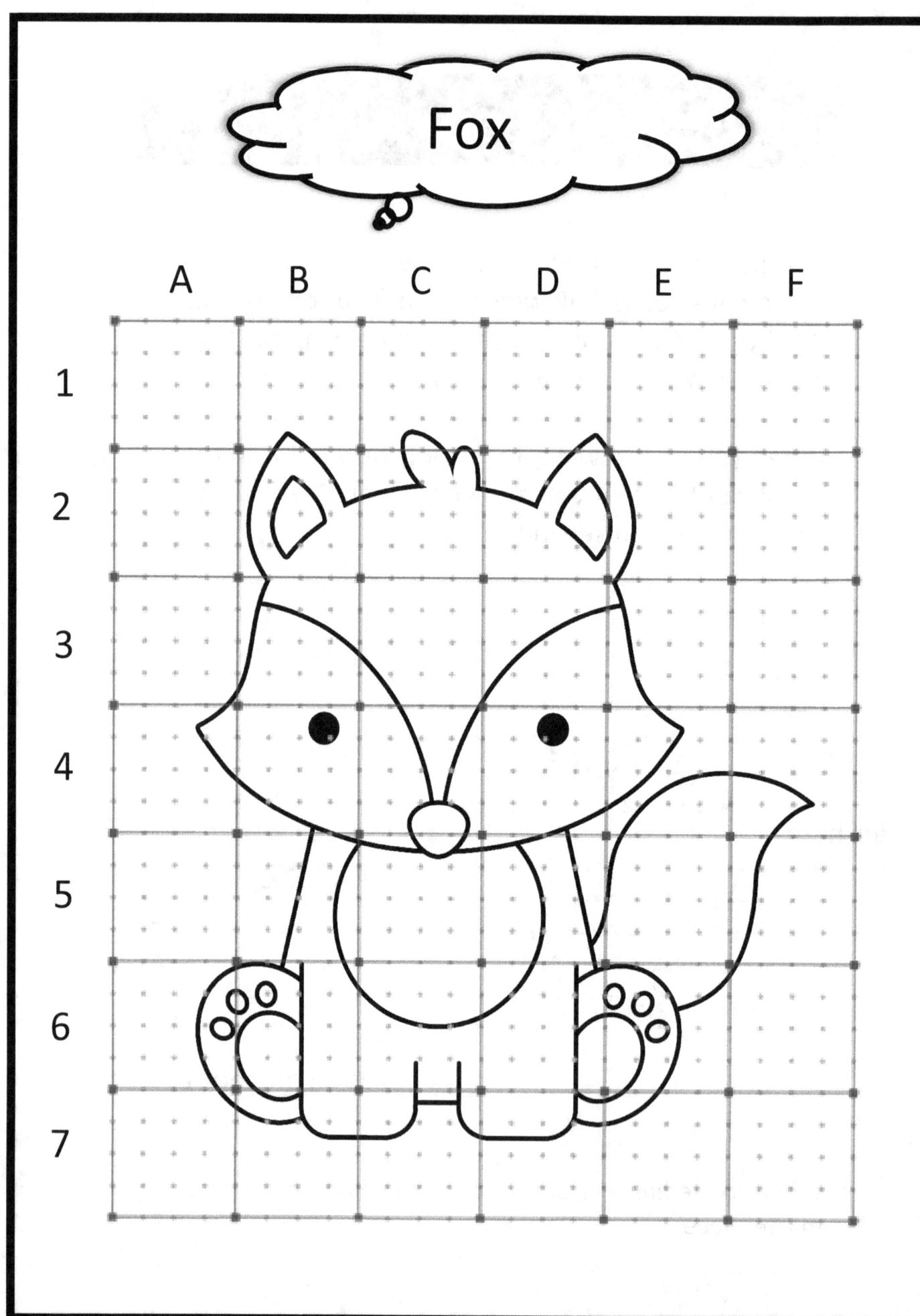

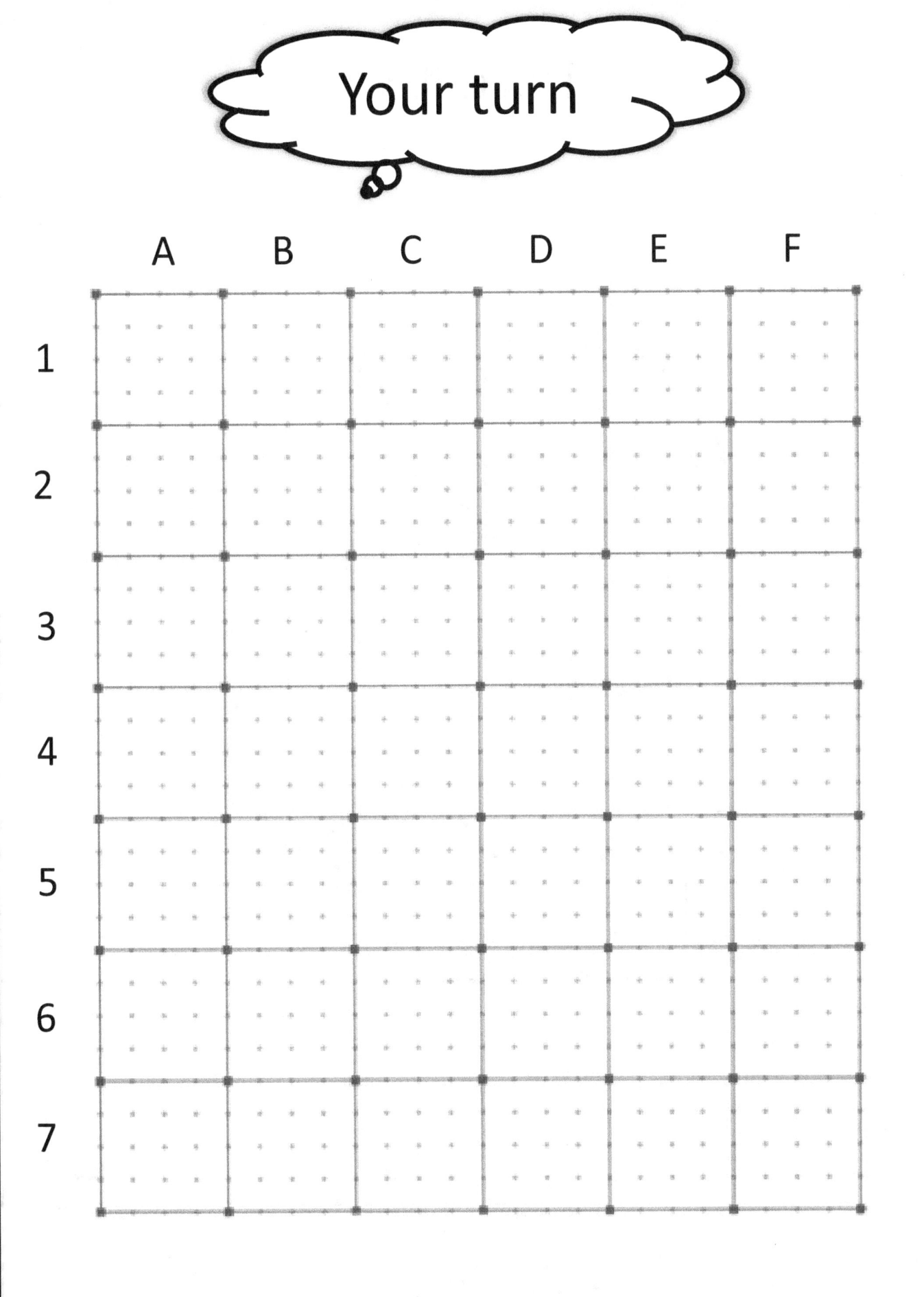

Trace It

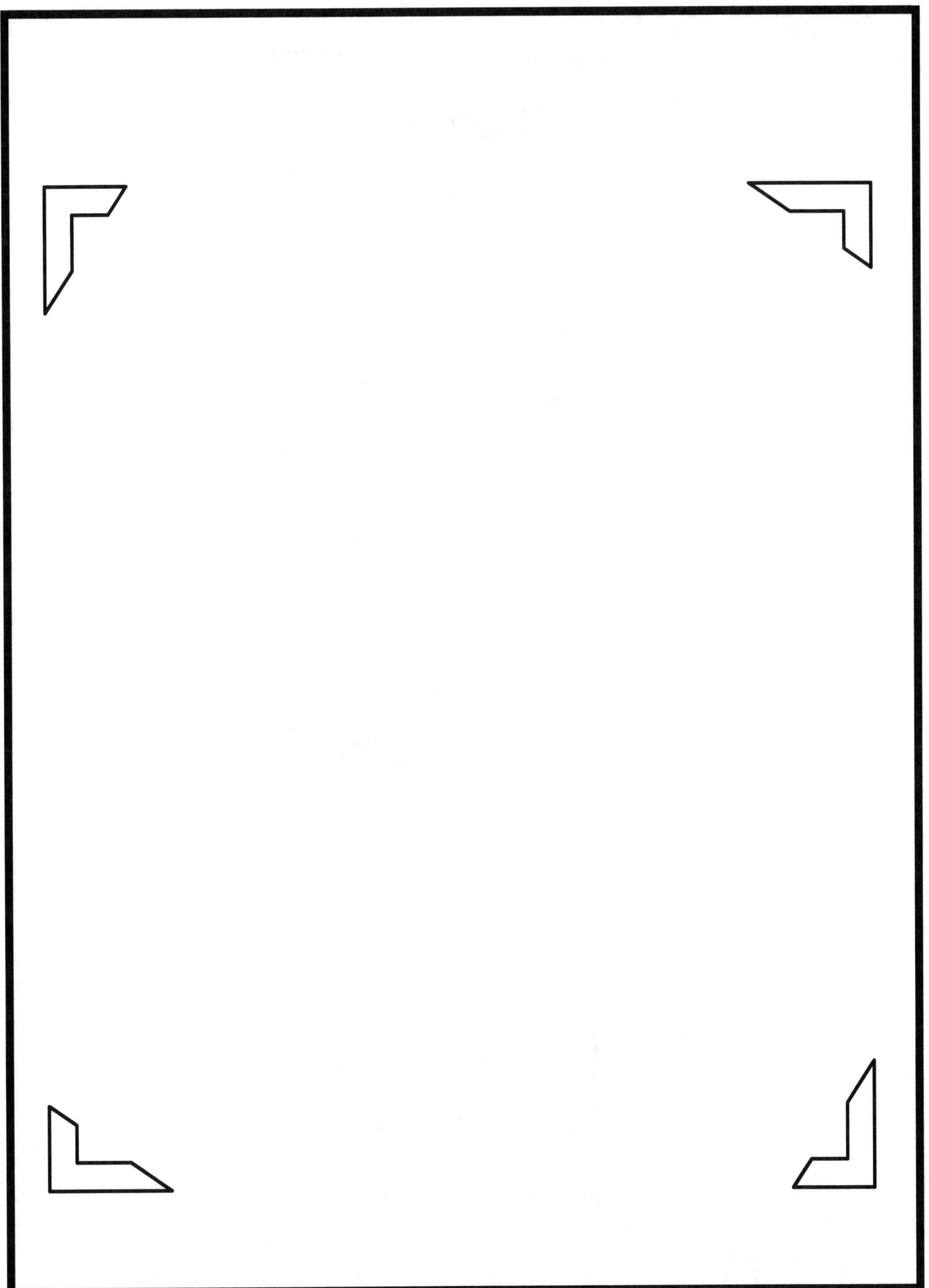

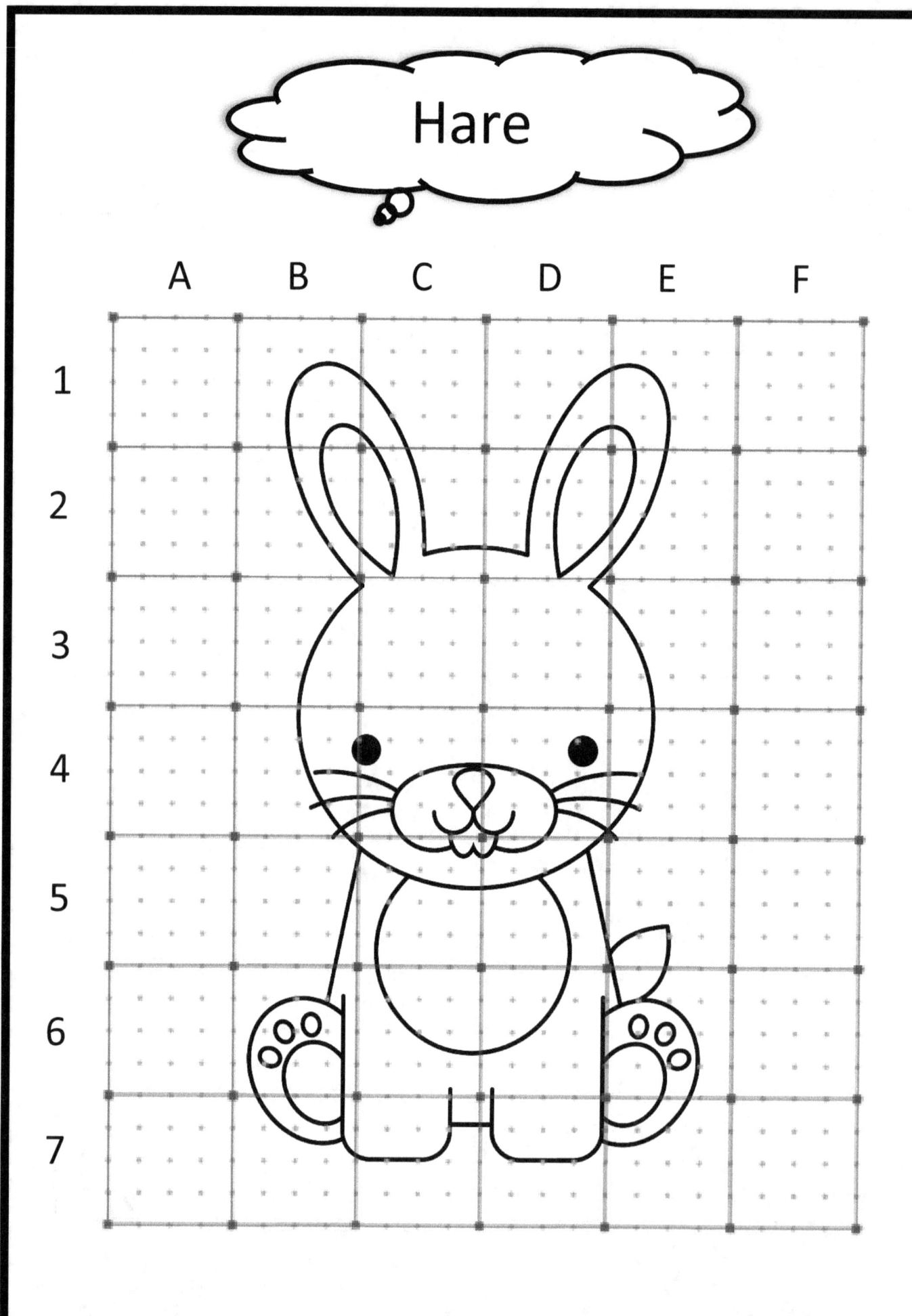

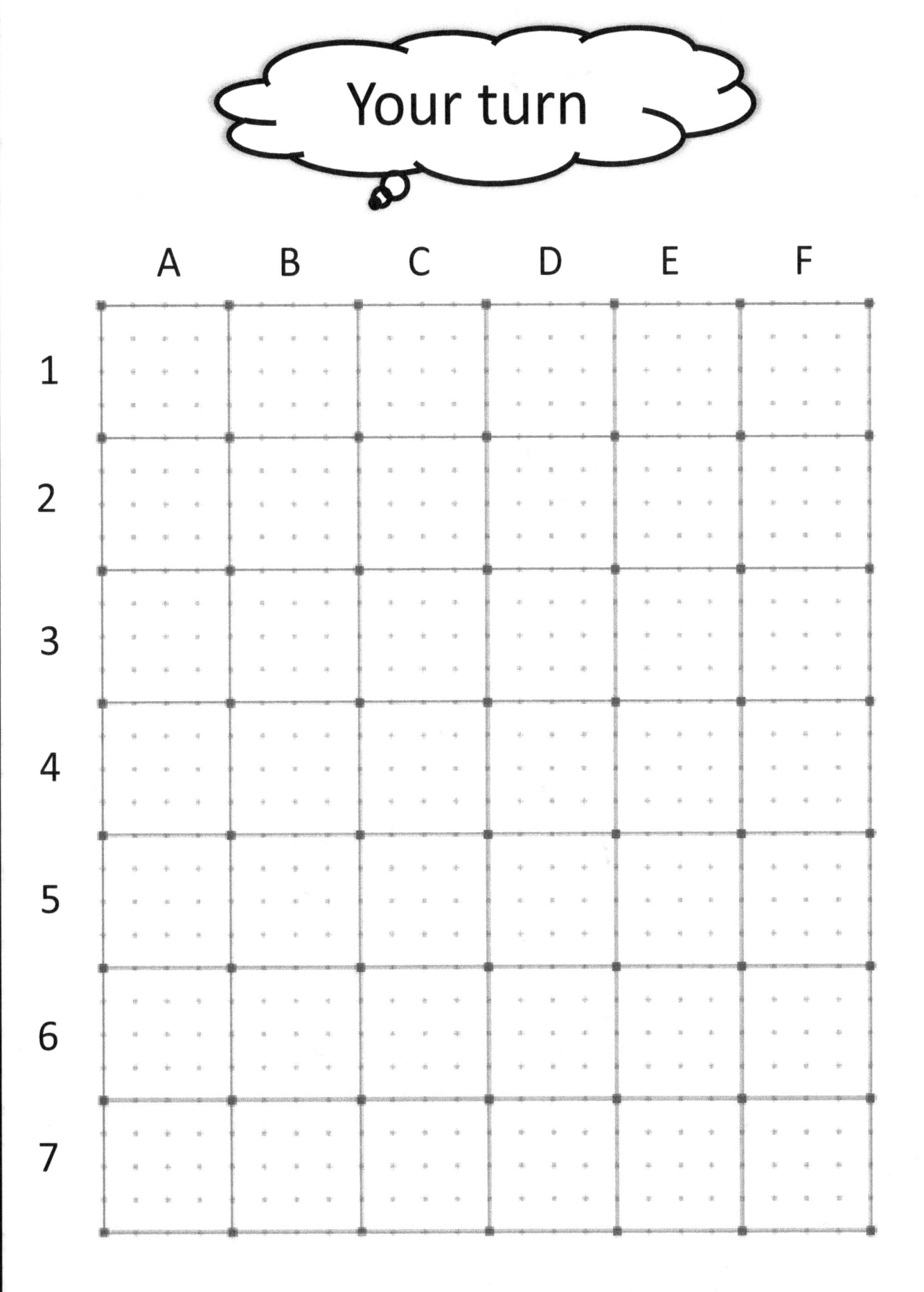

Trace It

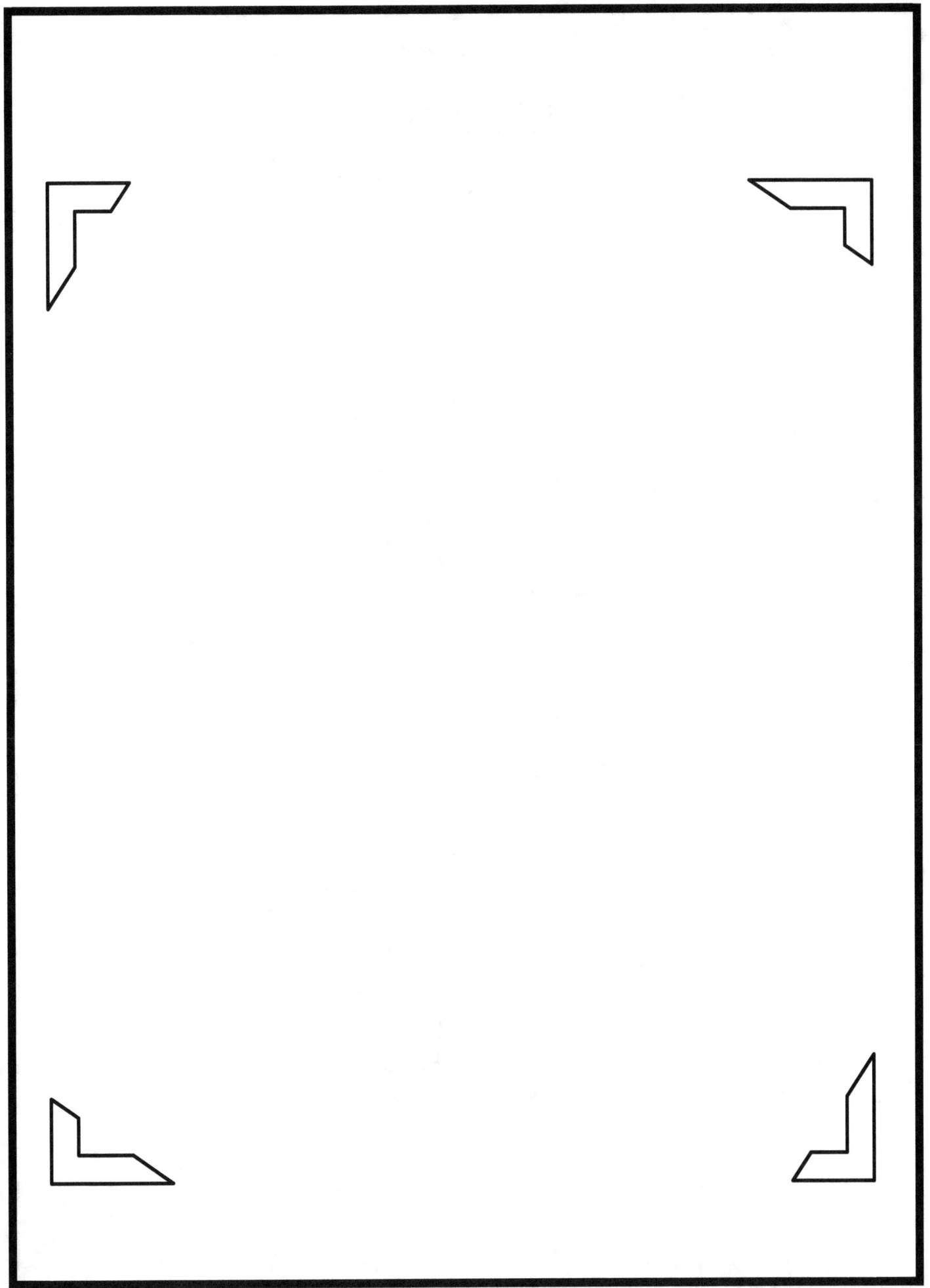

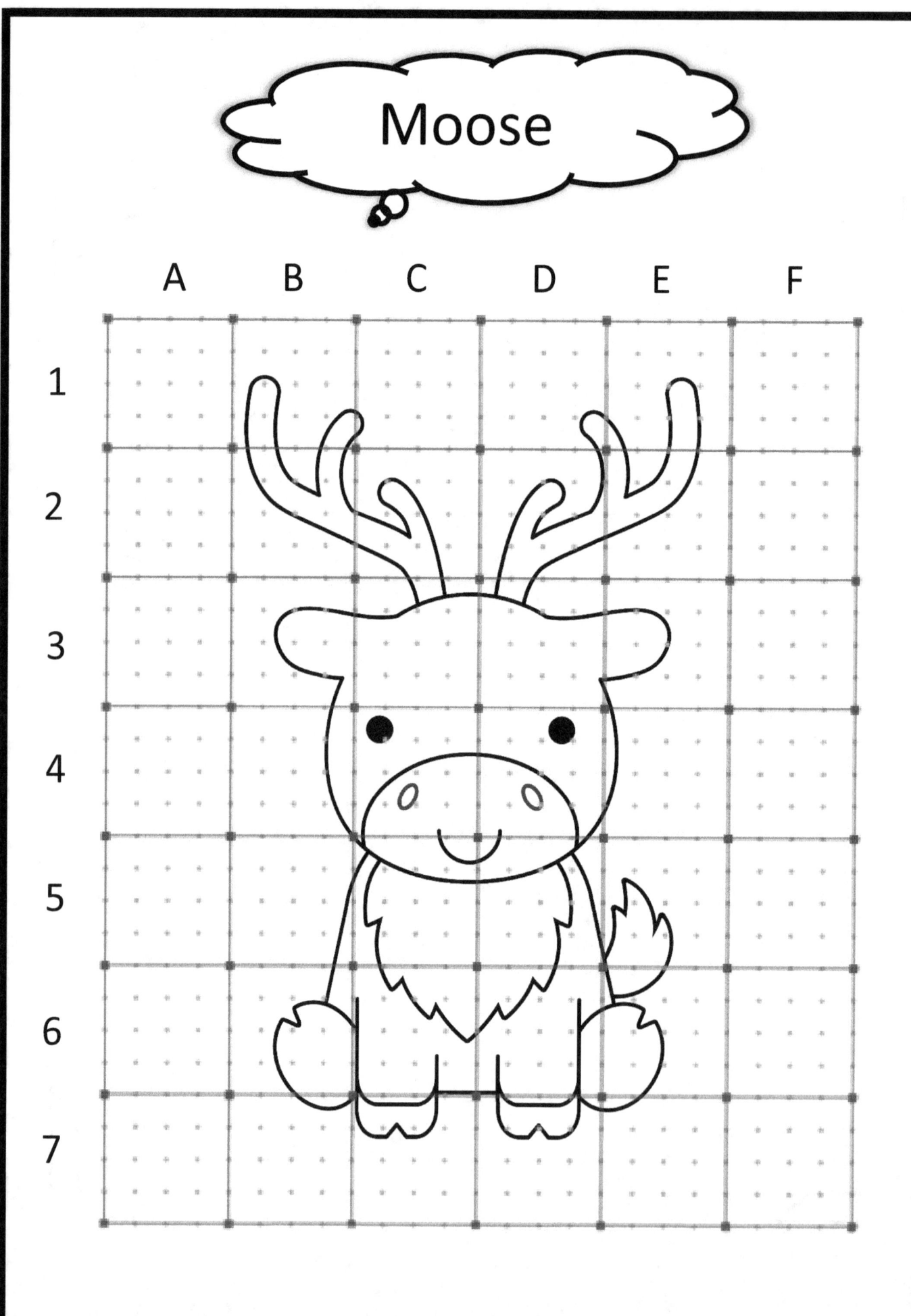

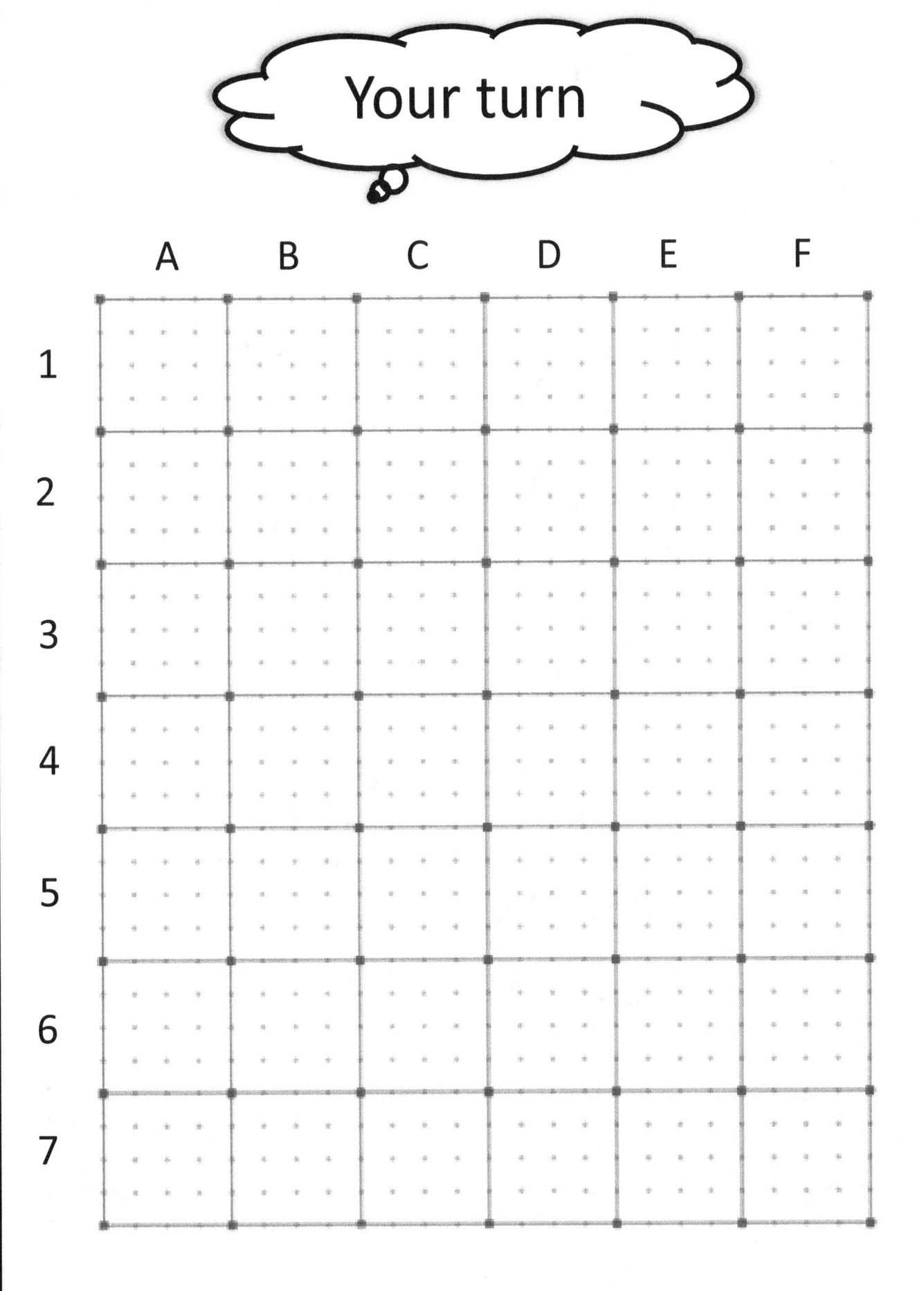

Trace It

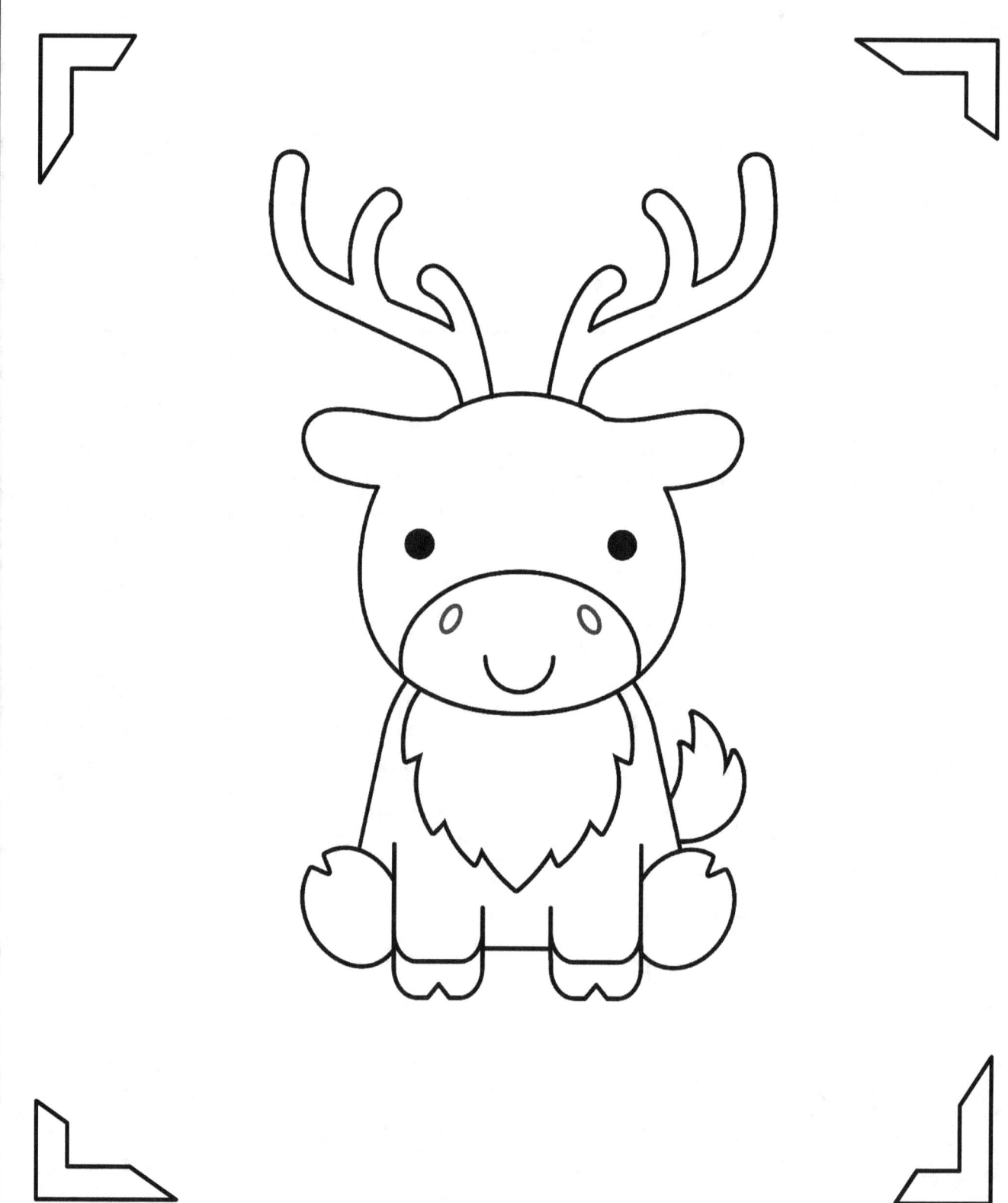

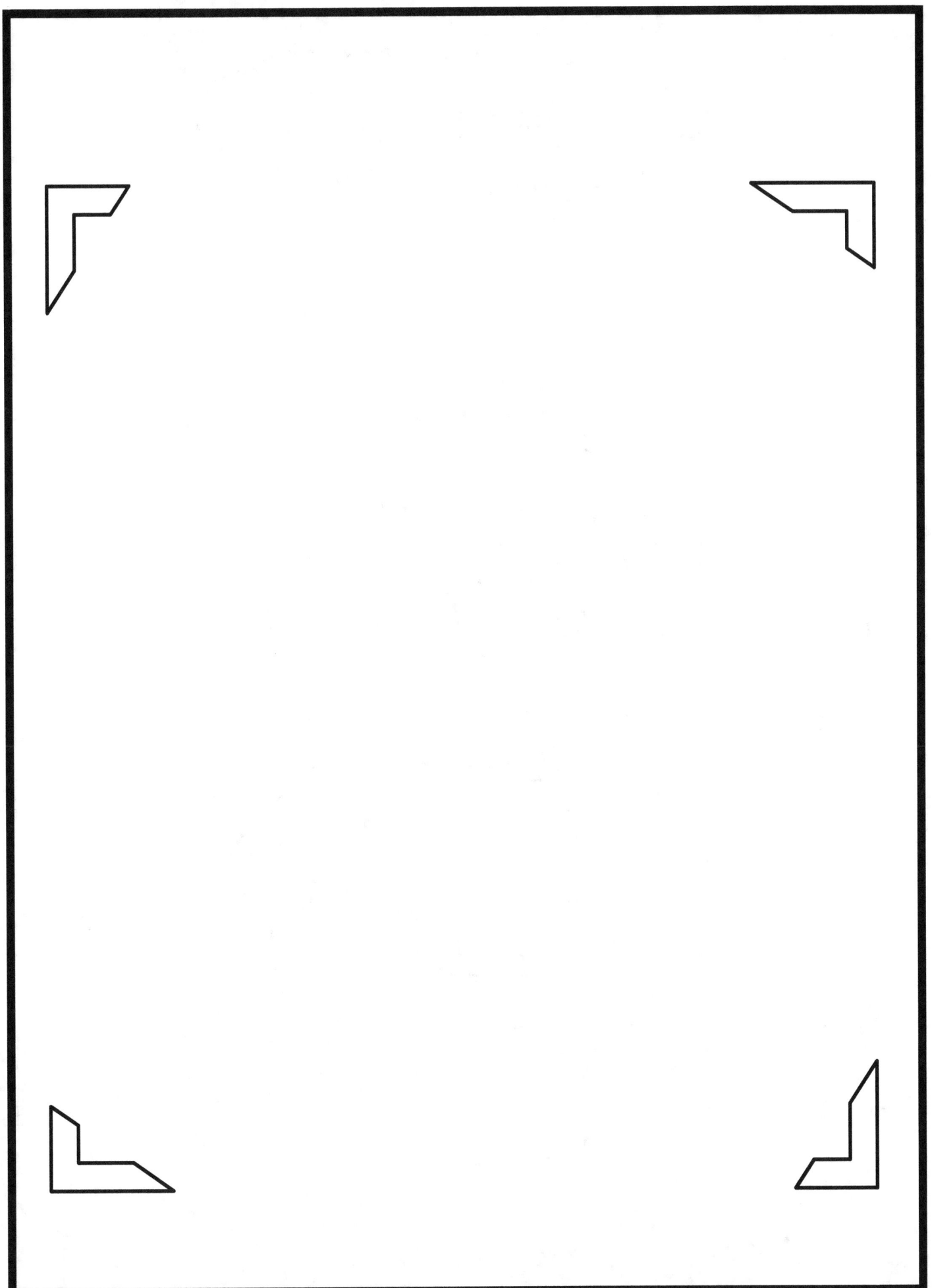

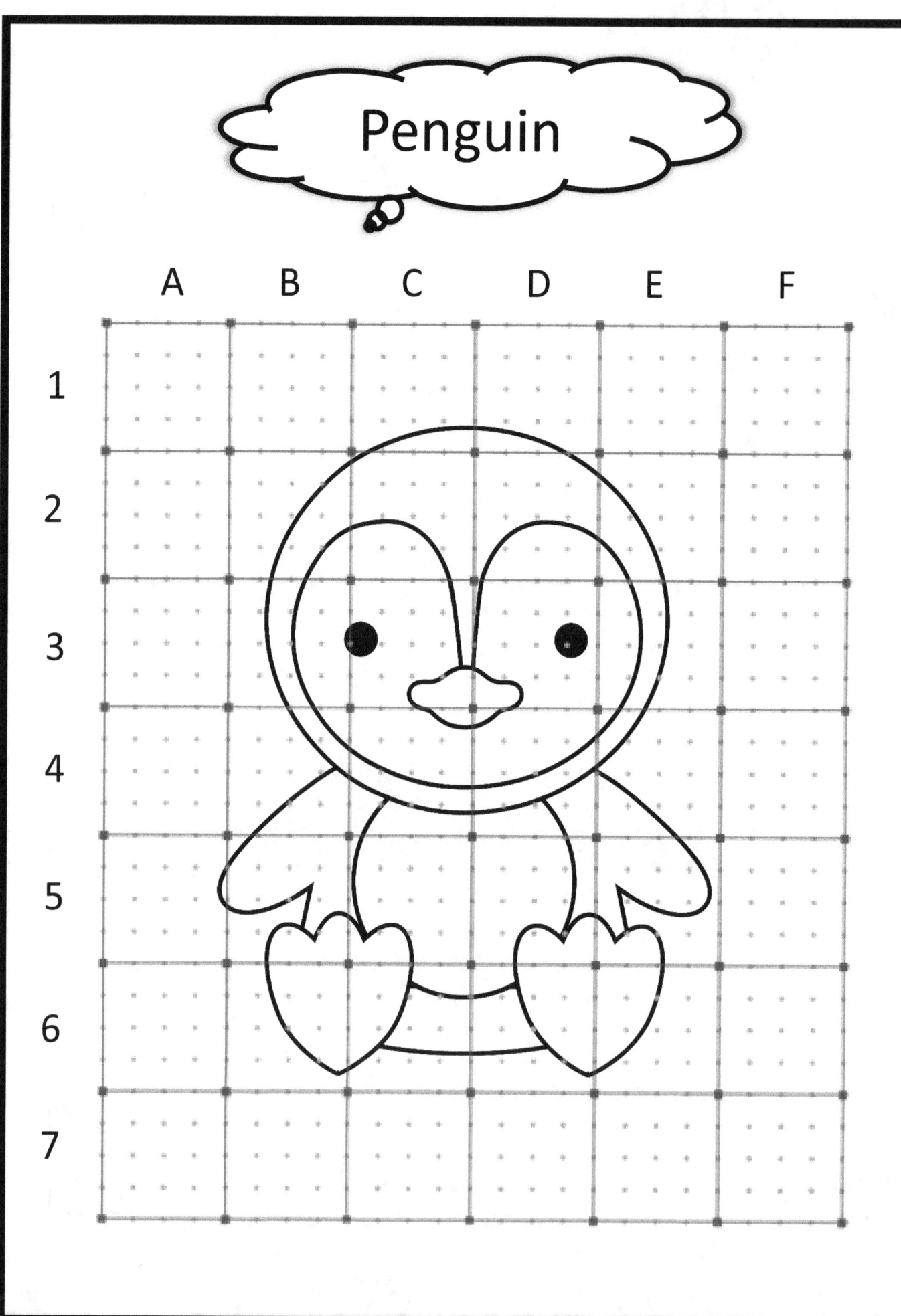

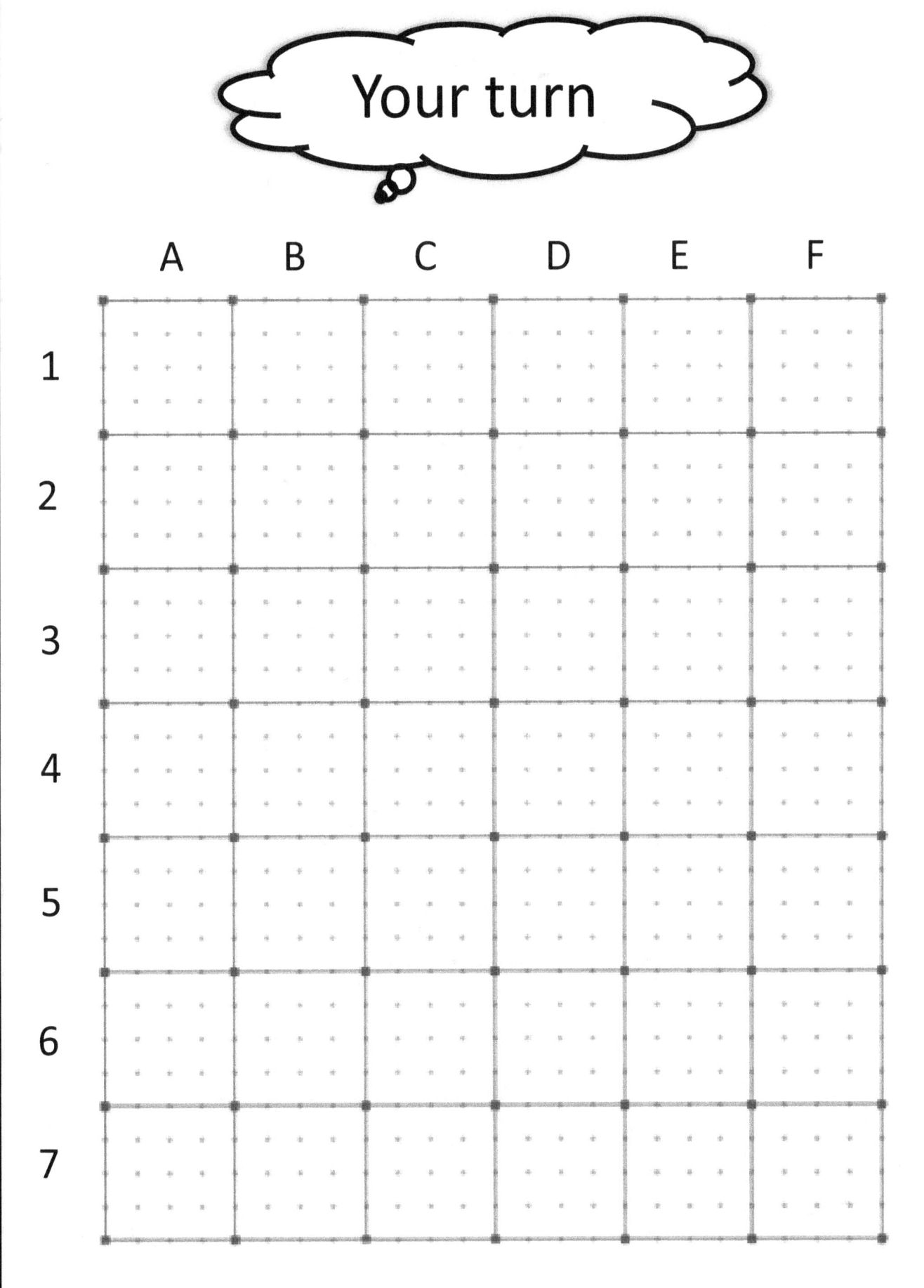

Trace It

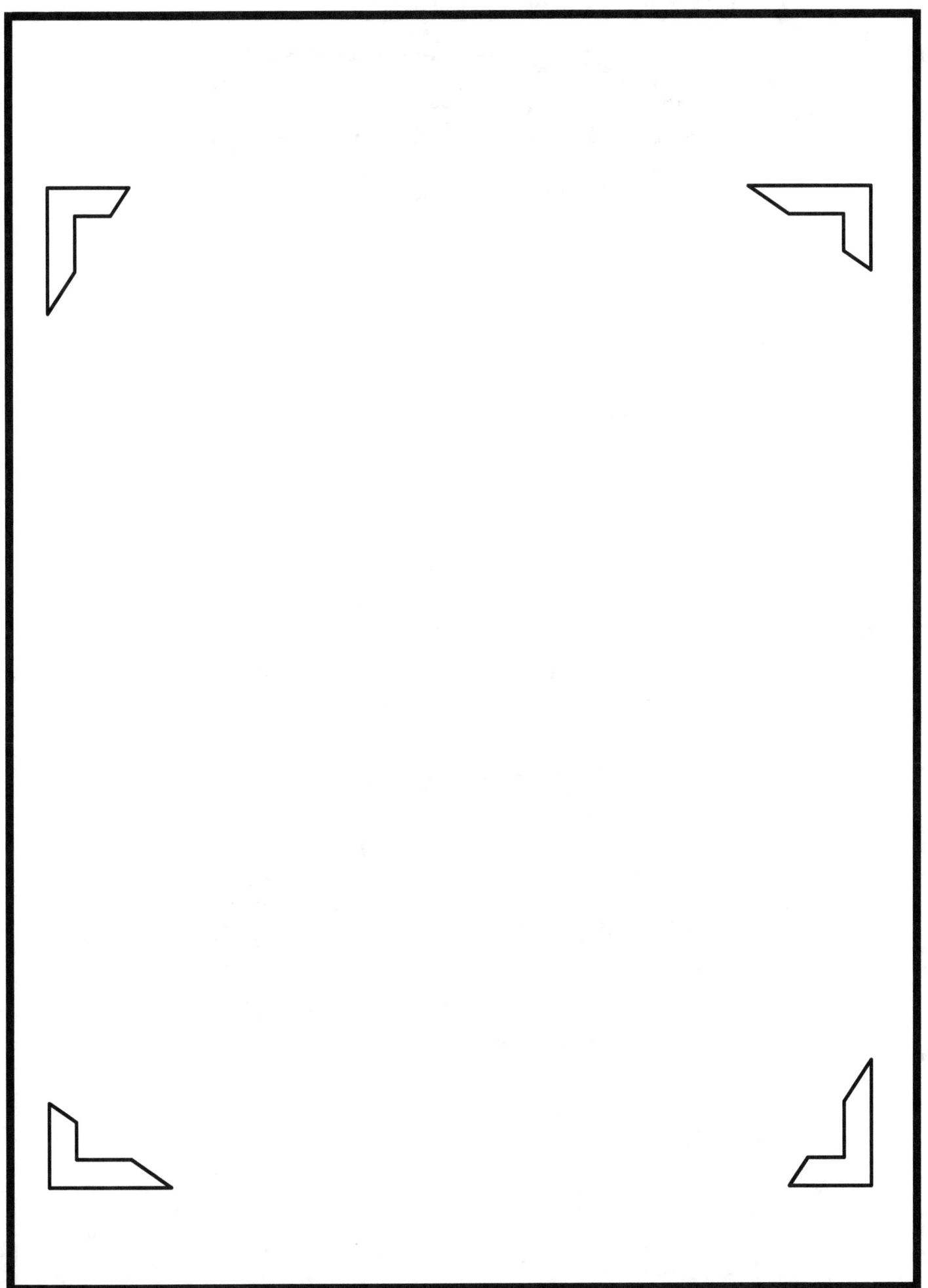

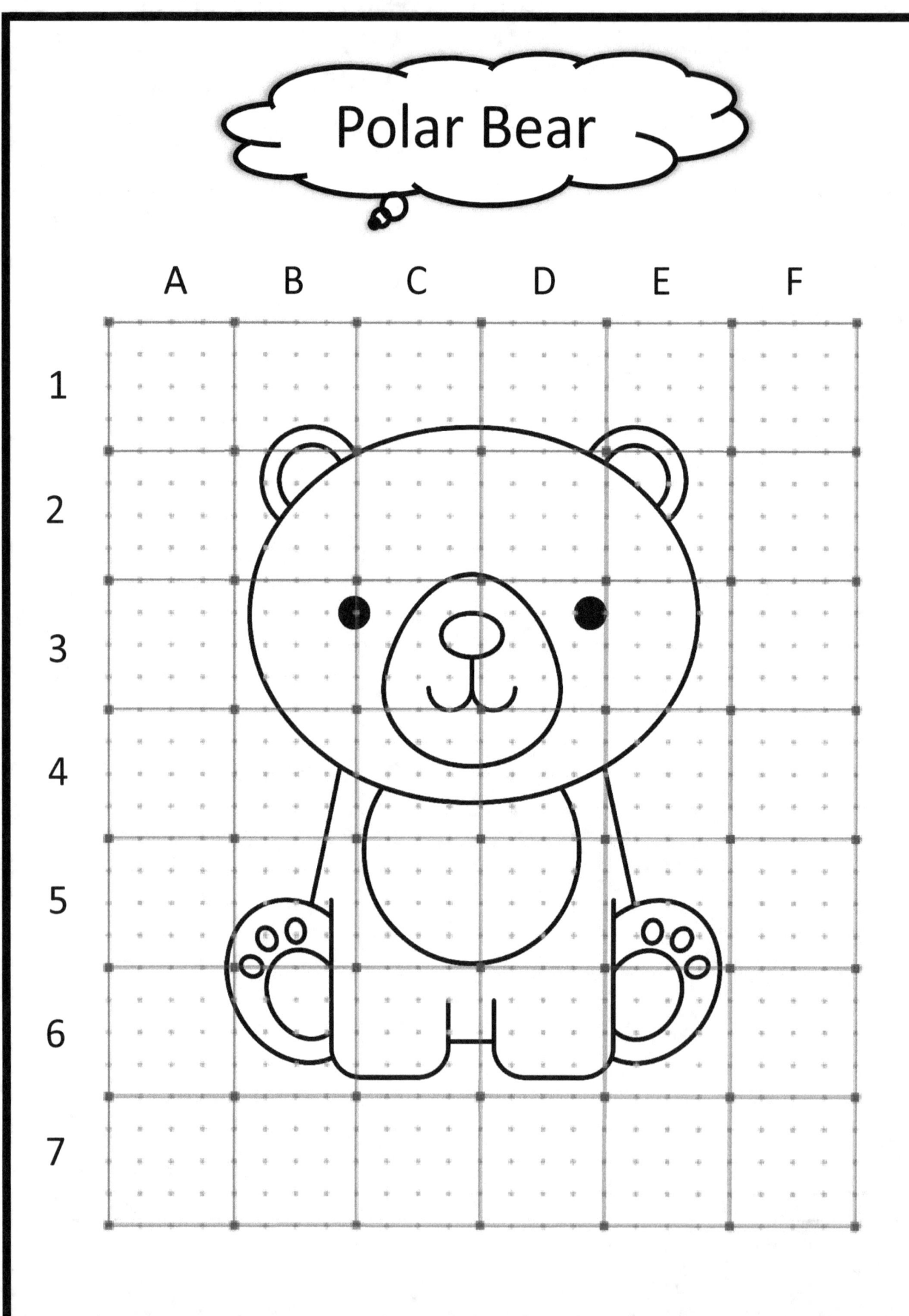

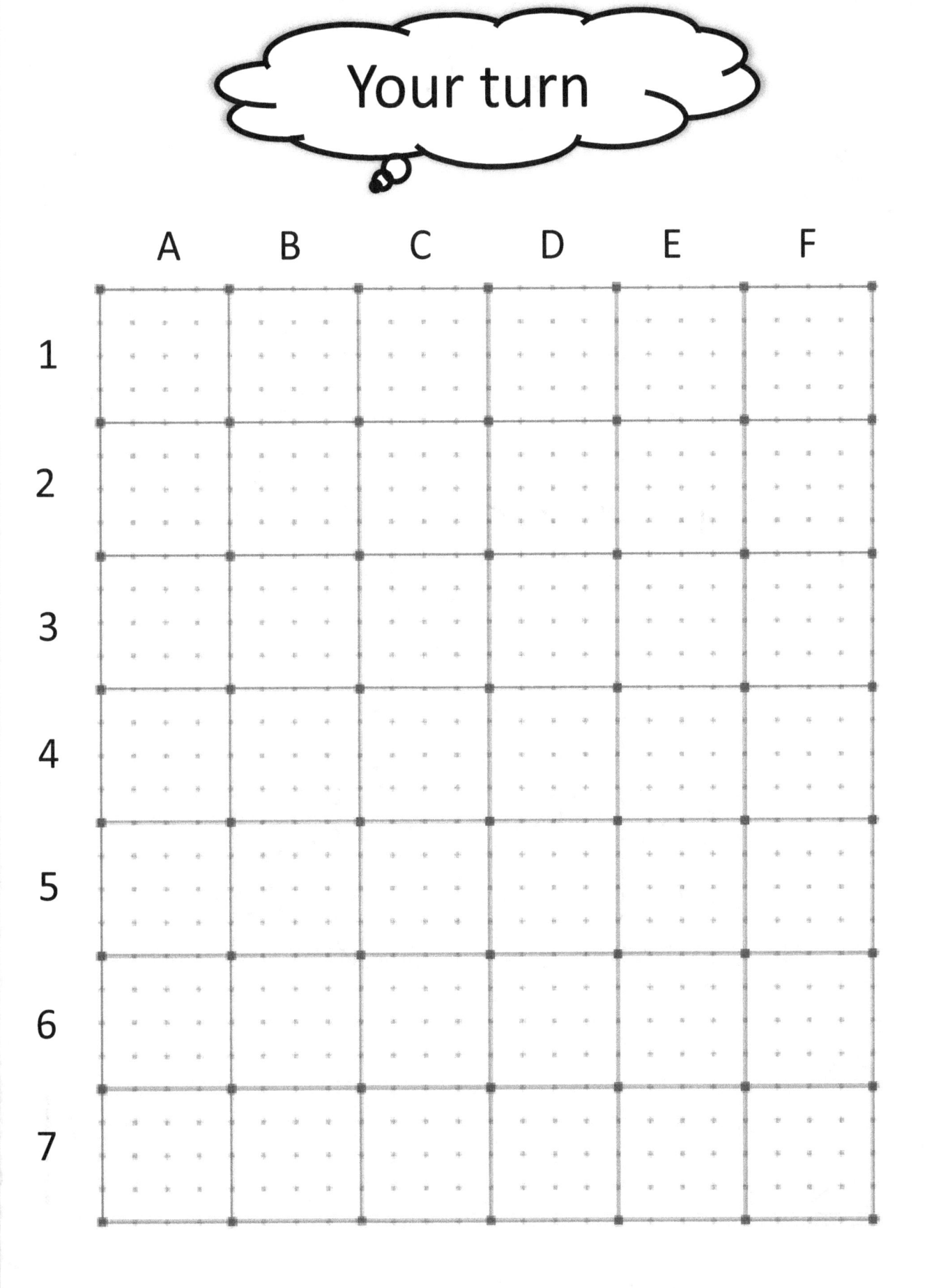

Trace It

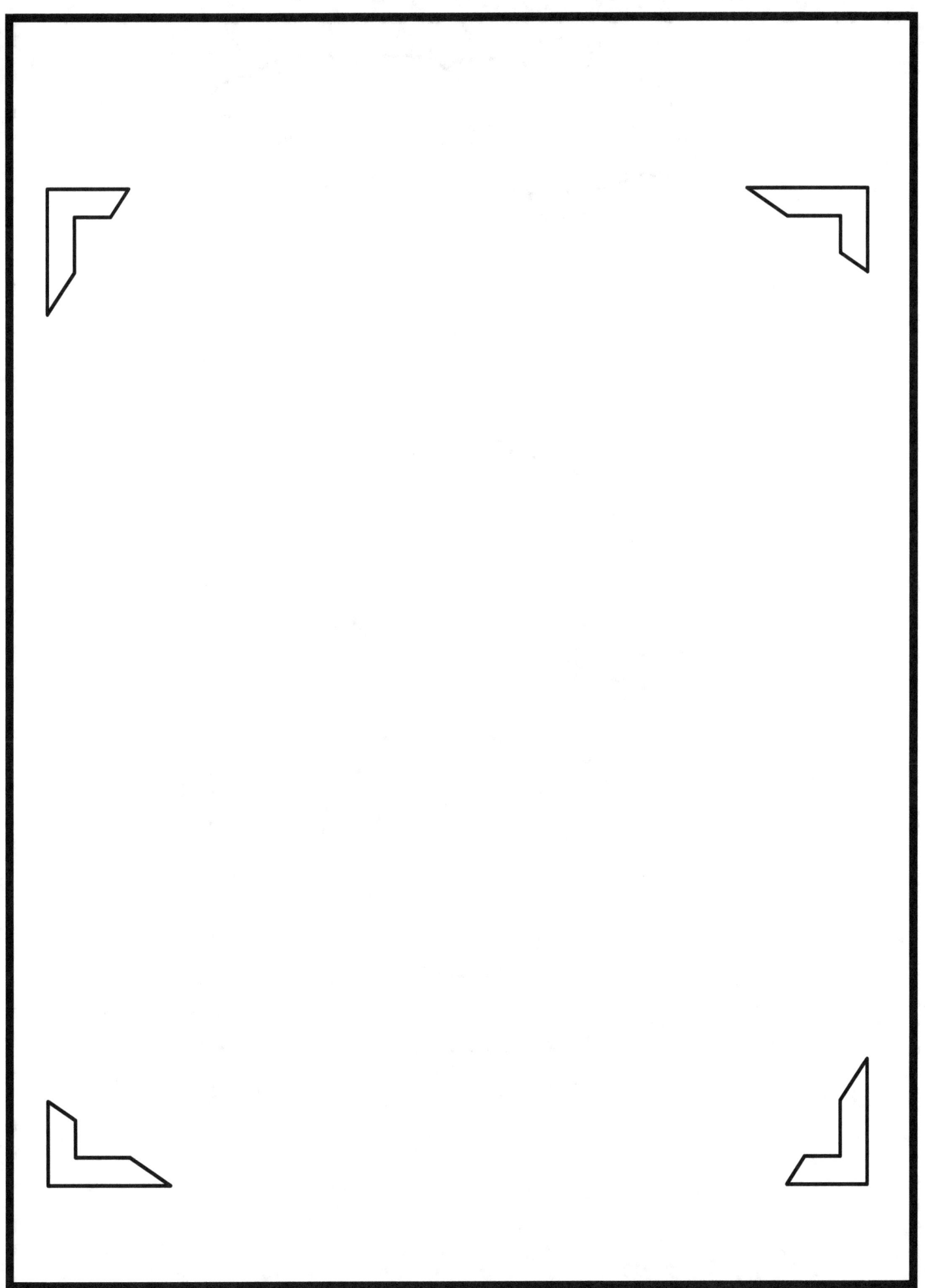

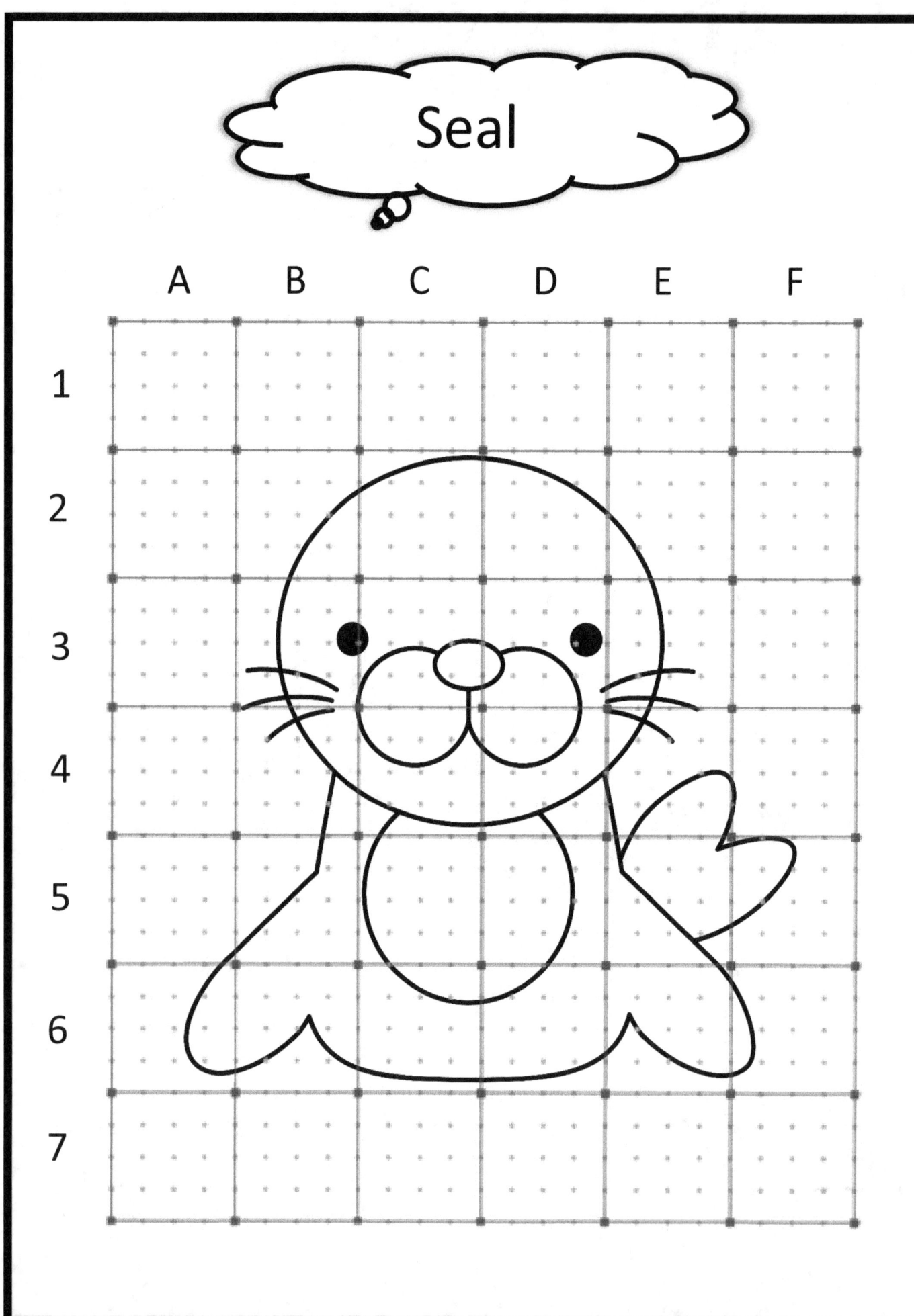

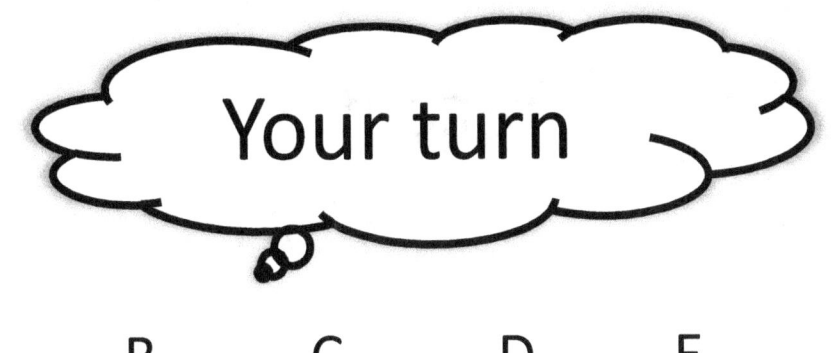

Trace It

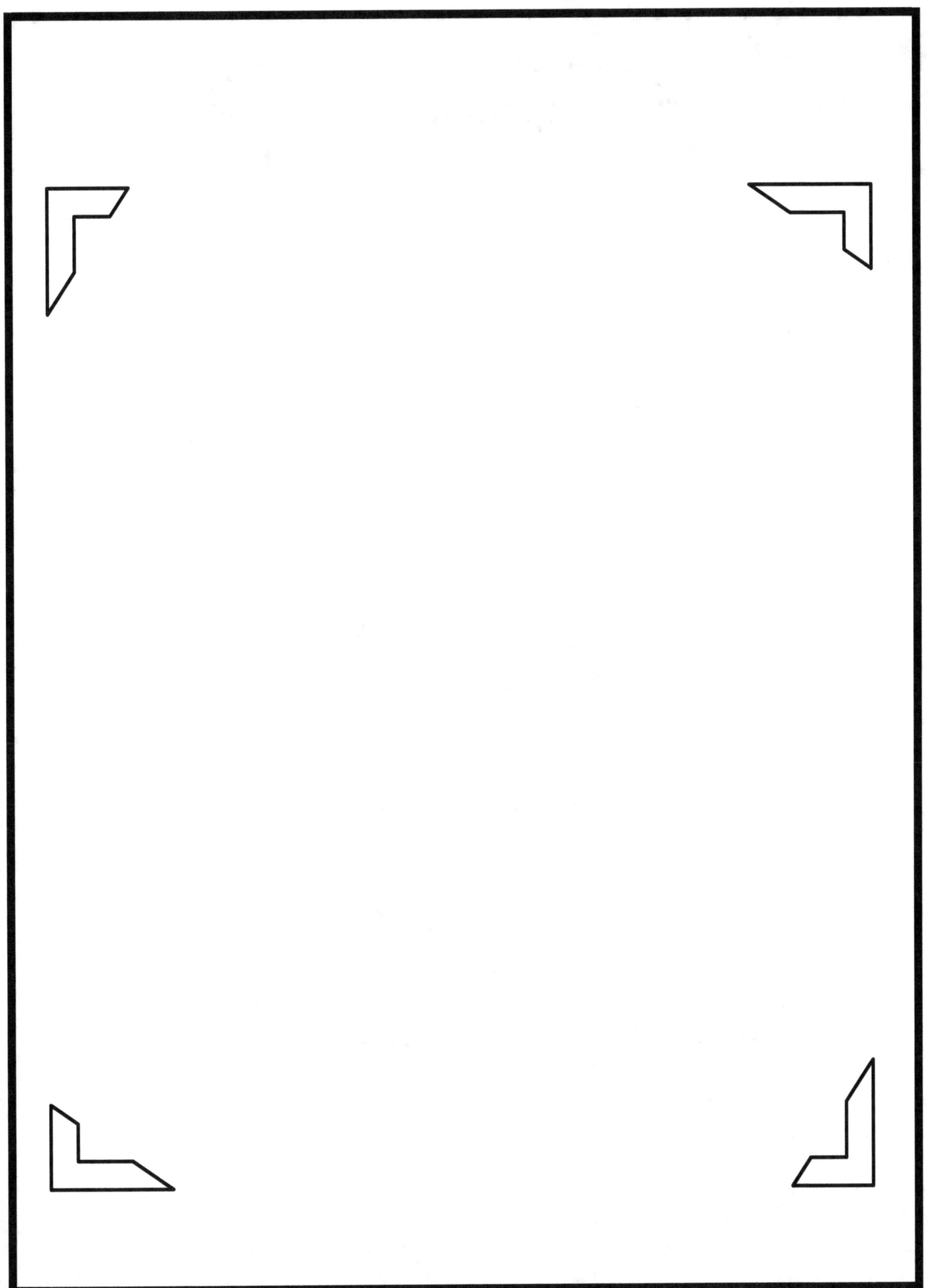

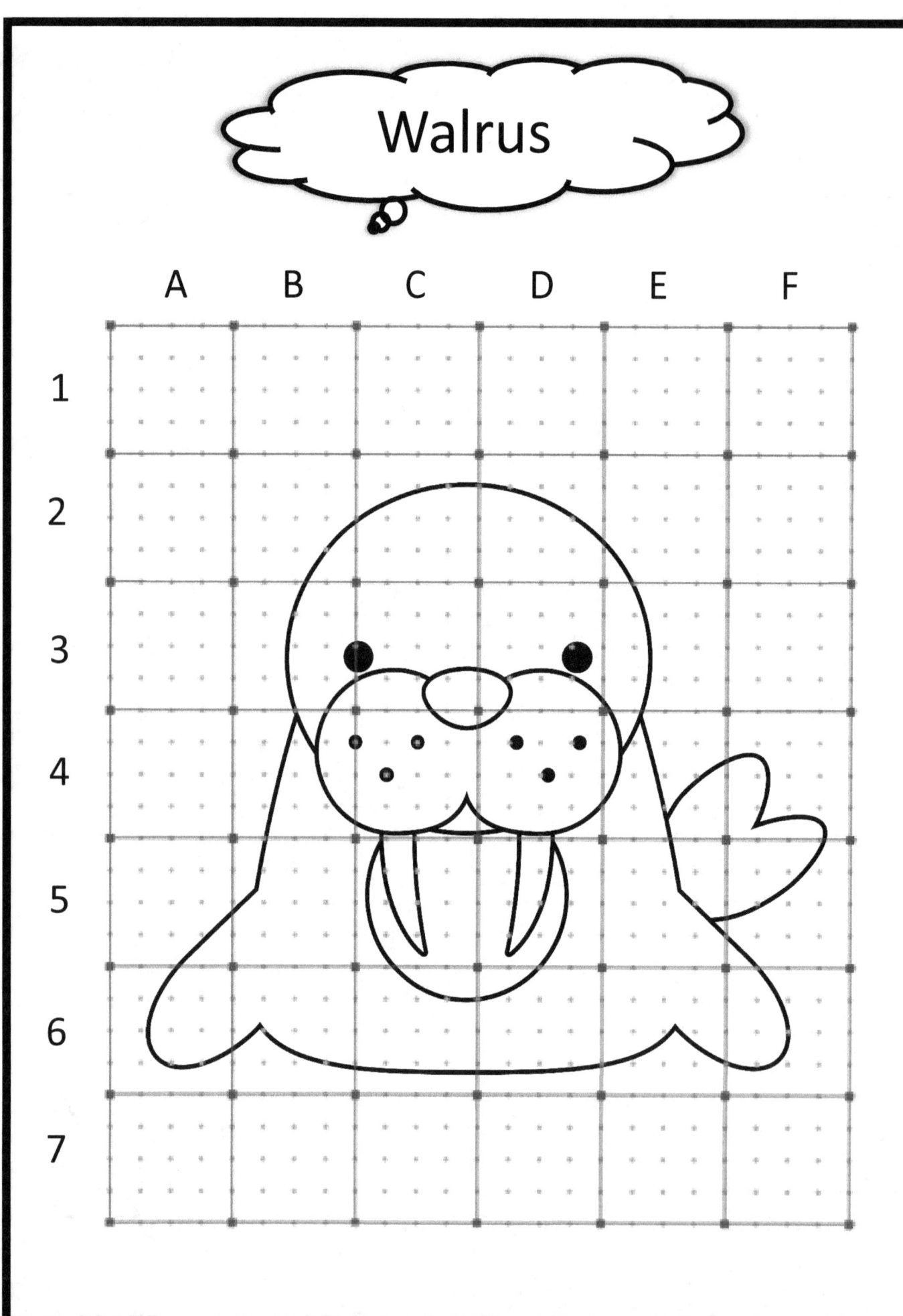

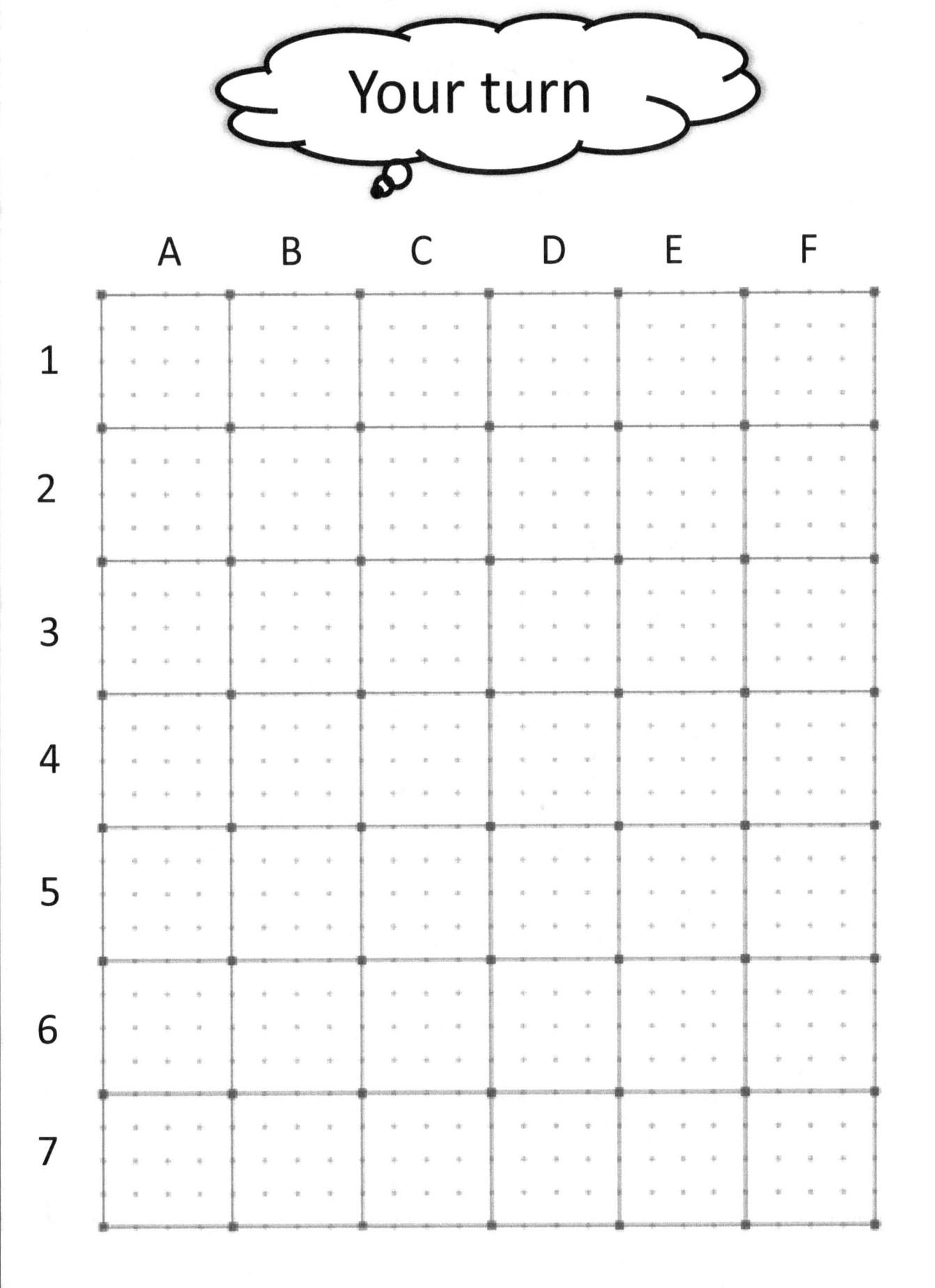

Trace It

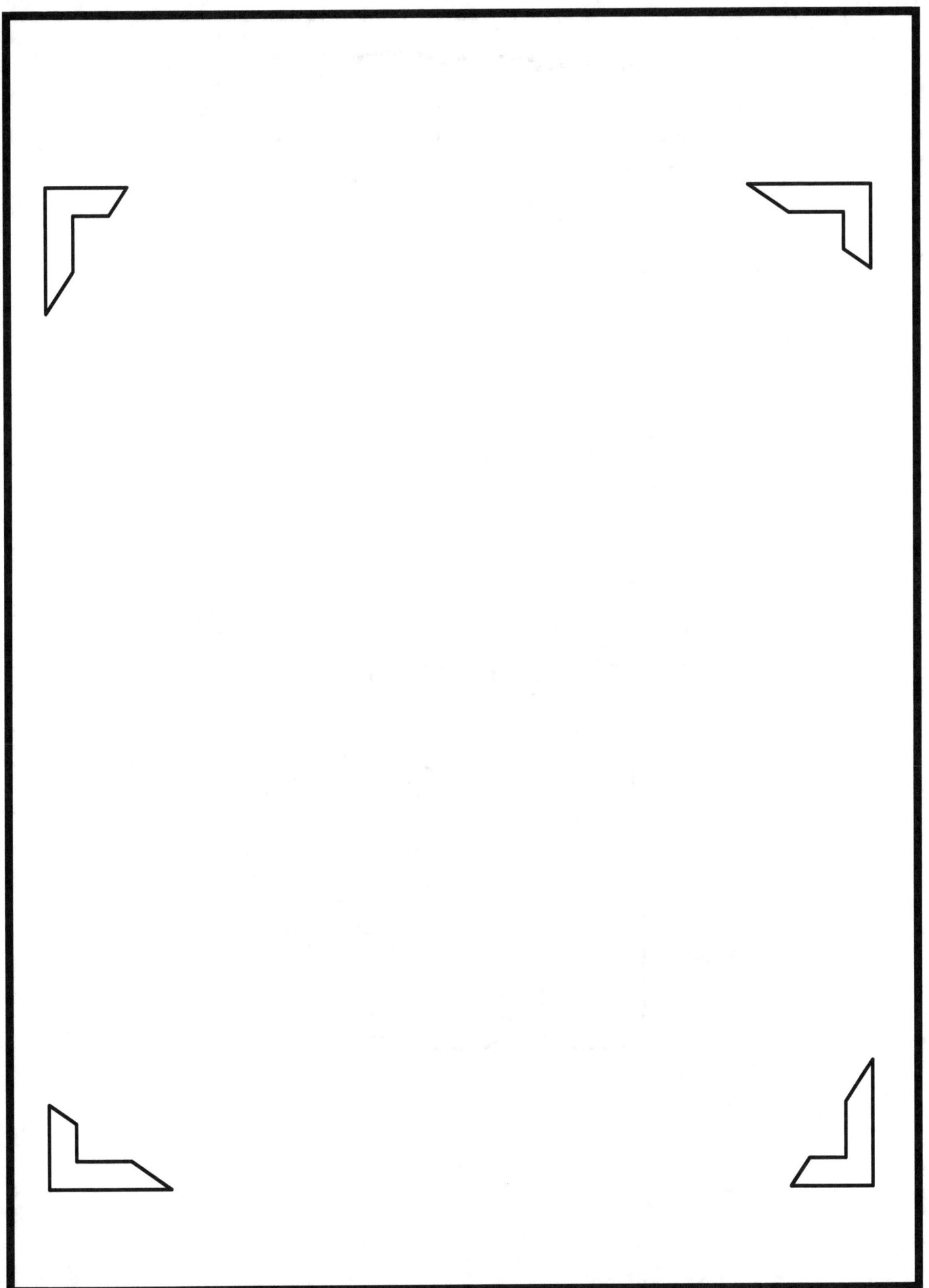

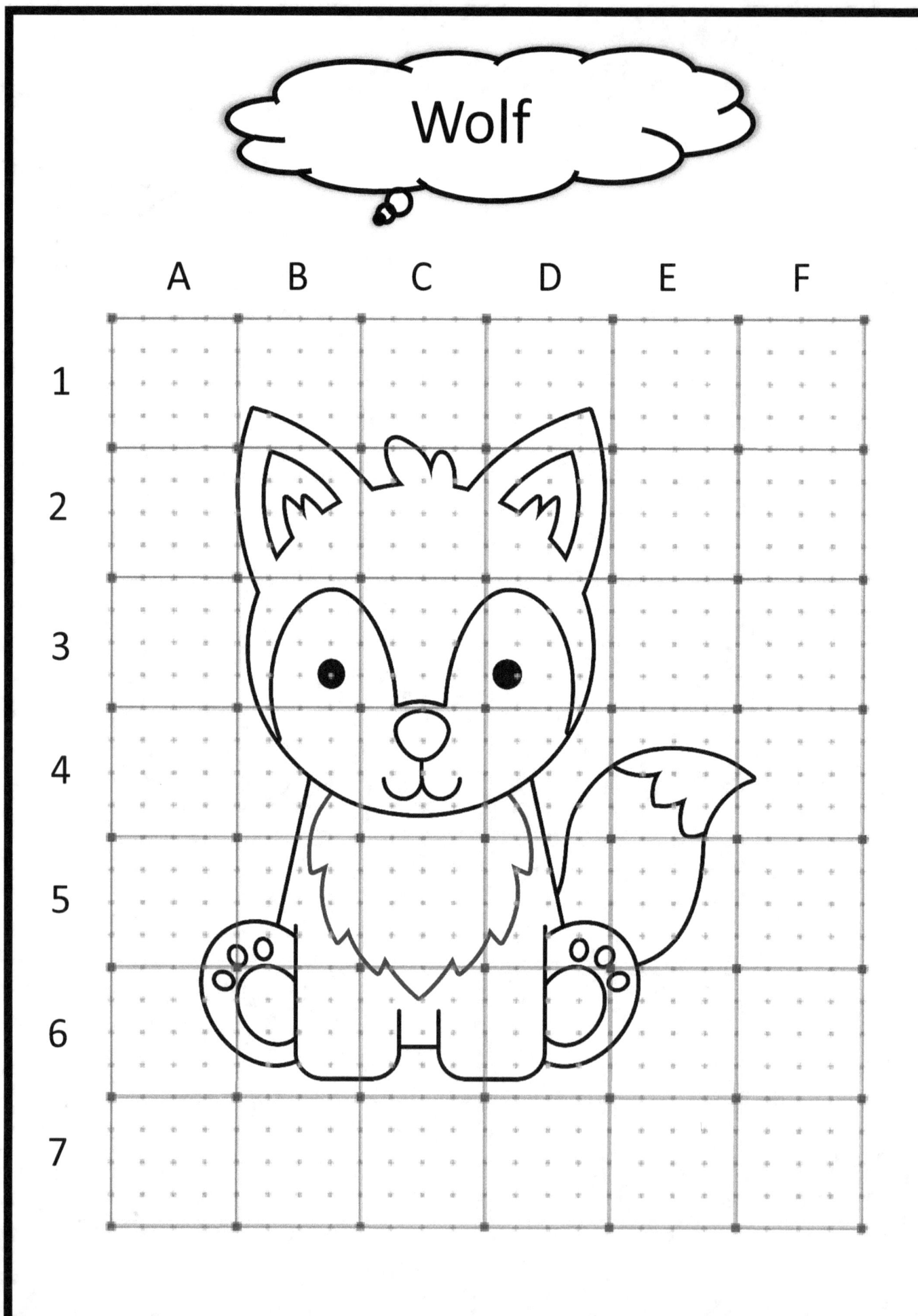

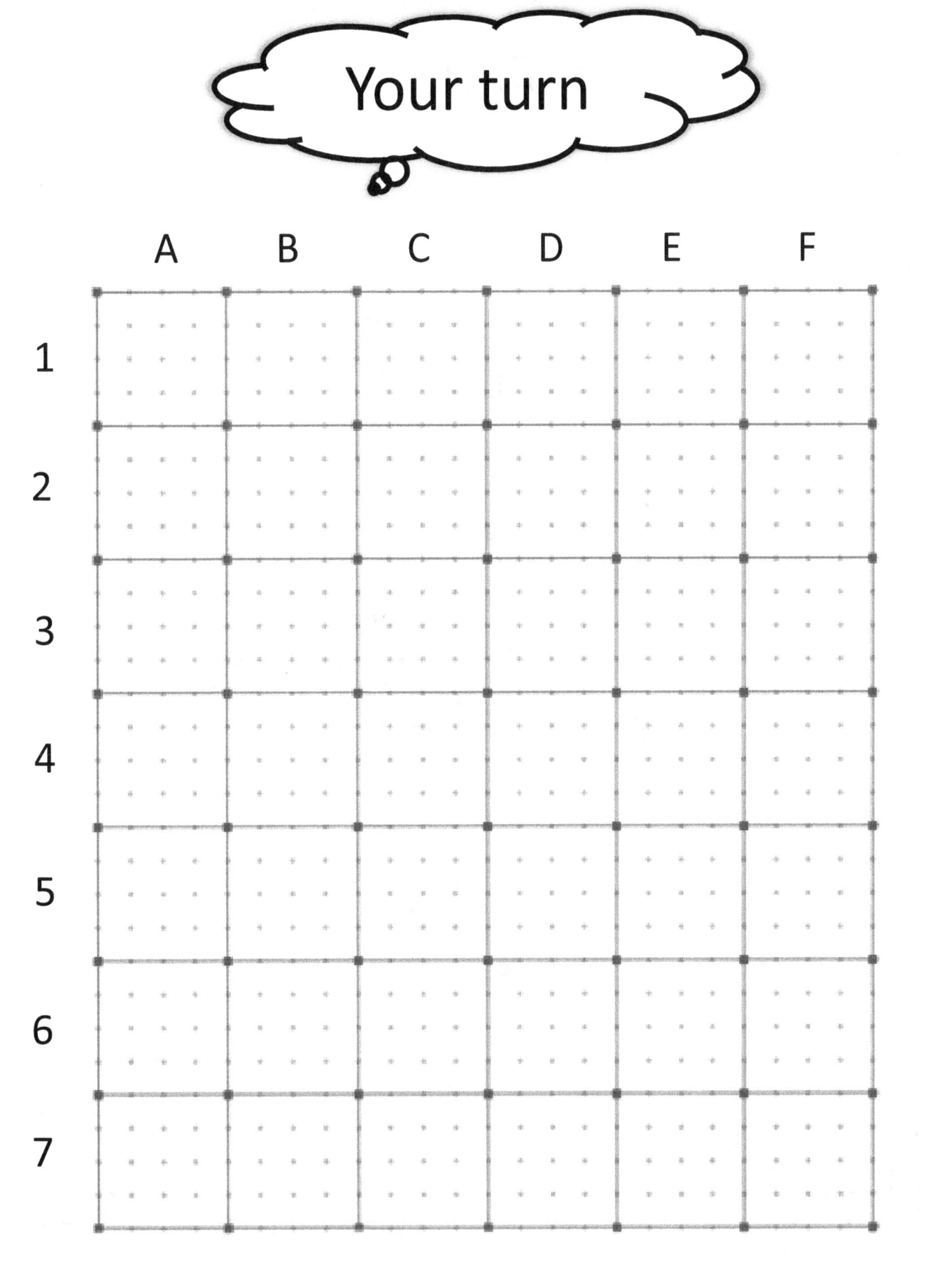

Trace It

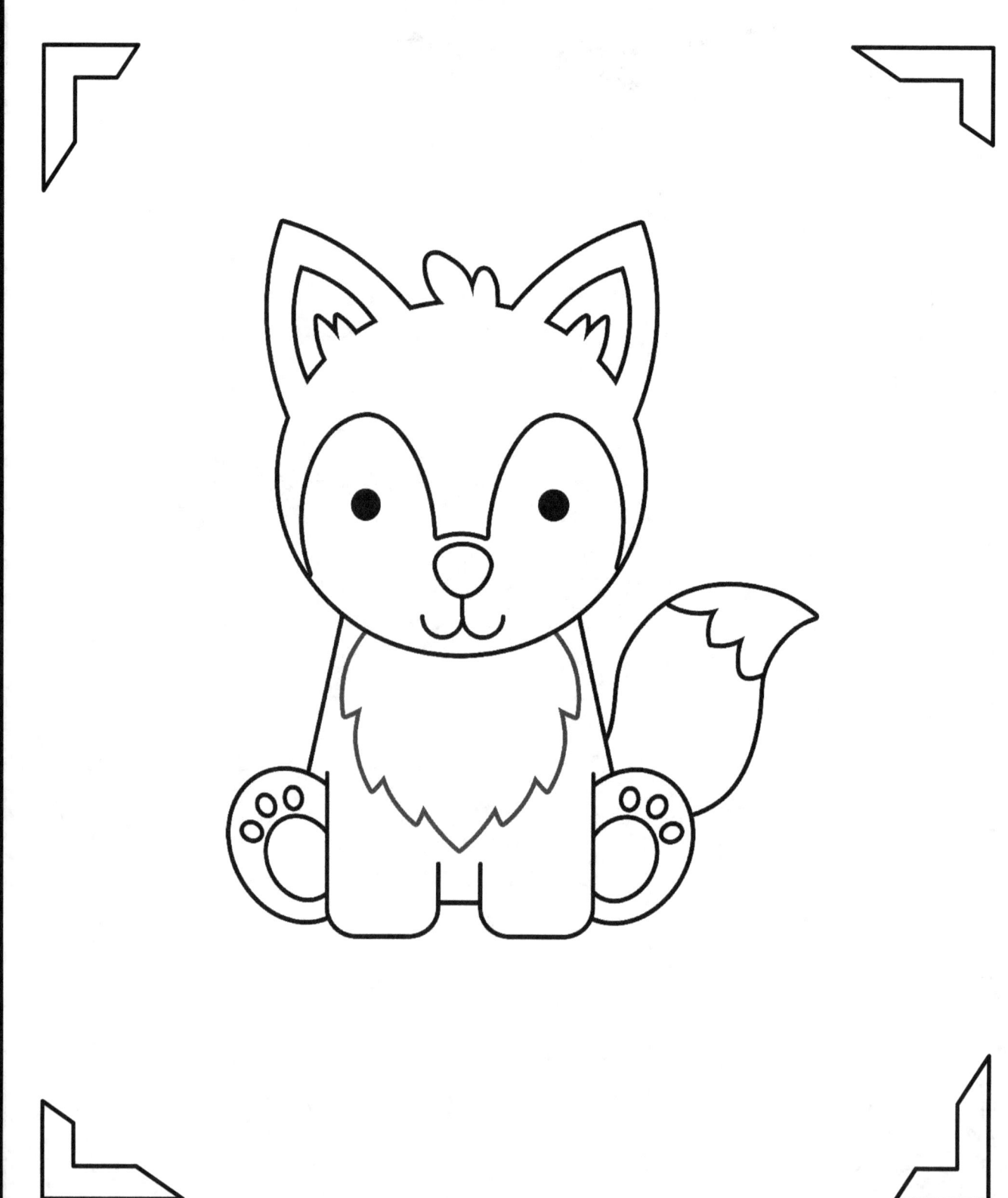

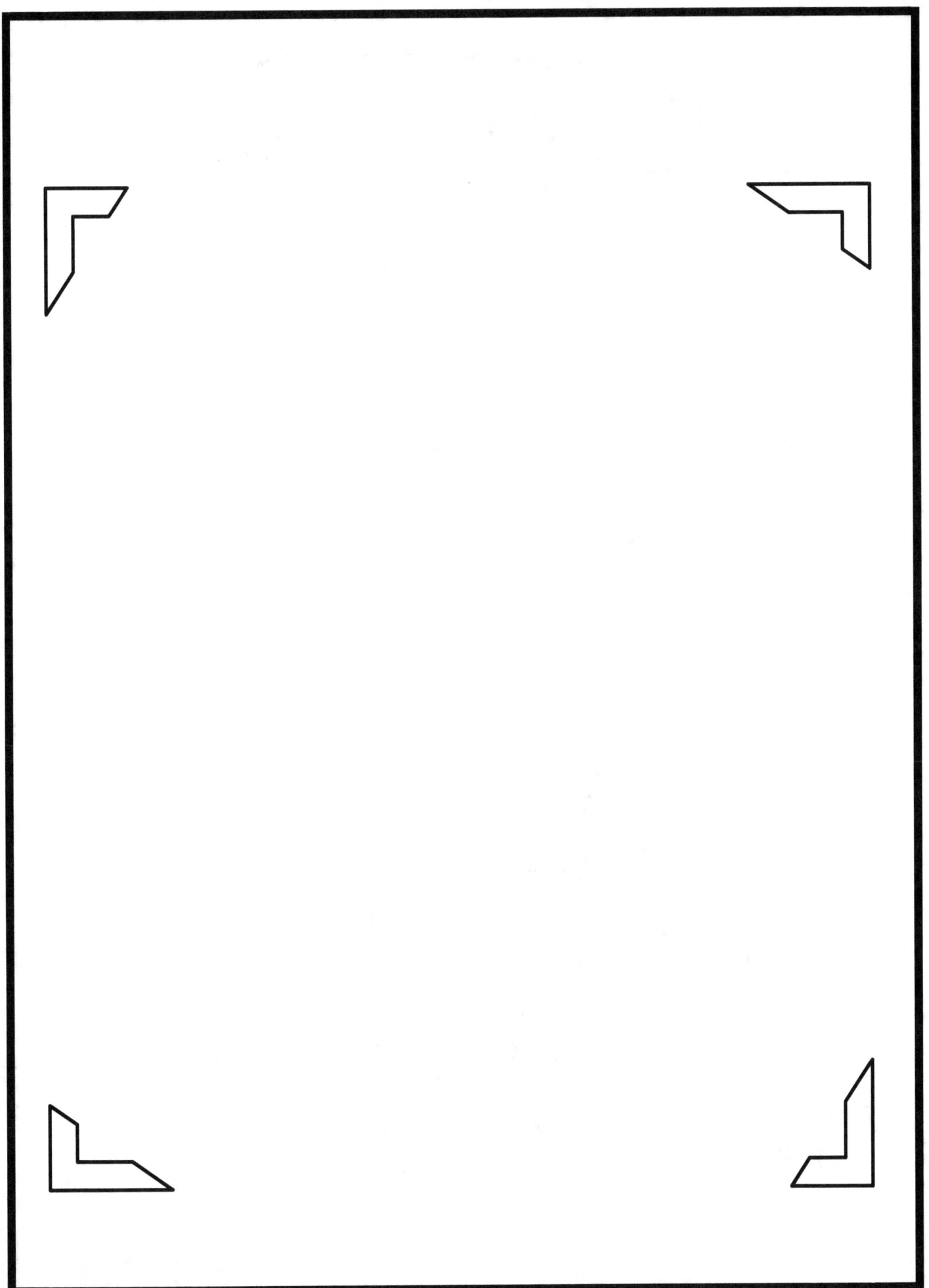

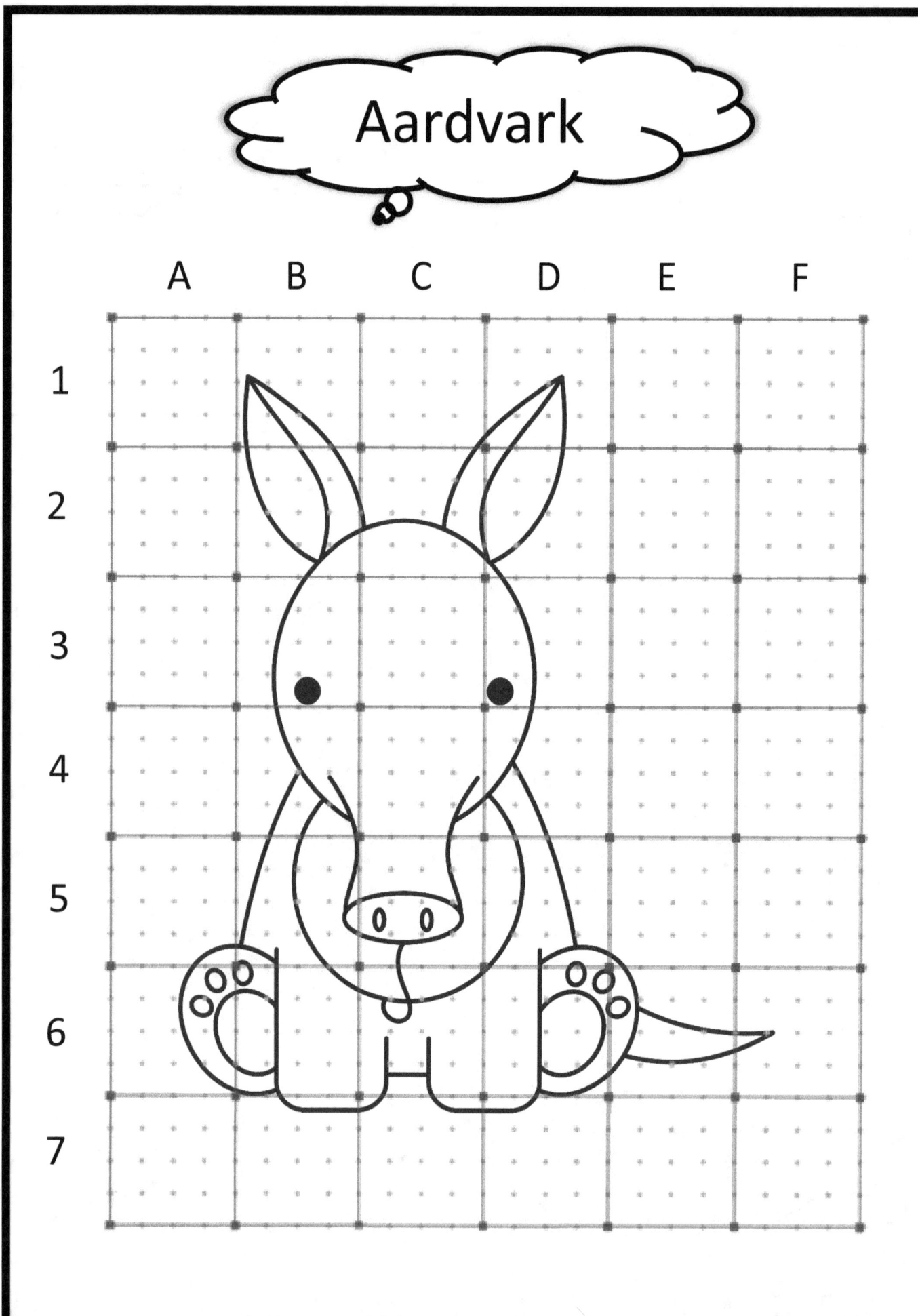

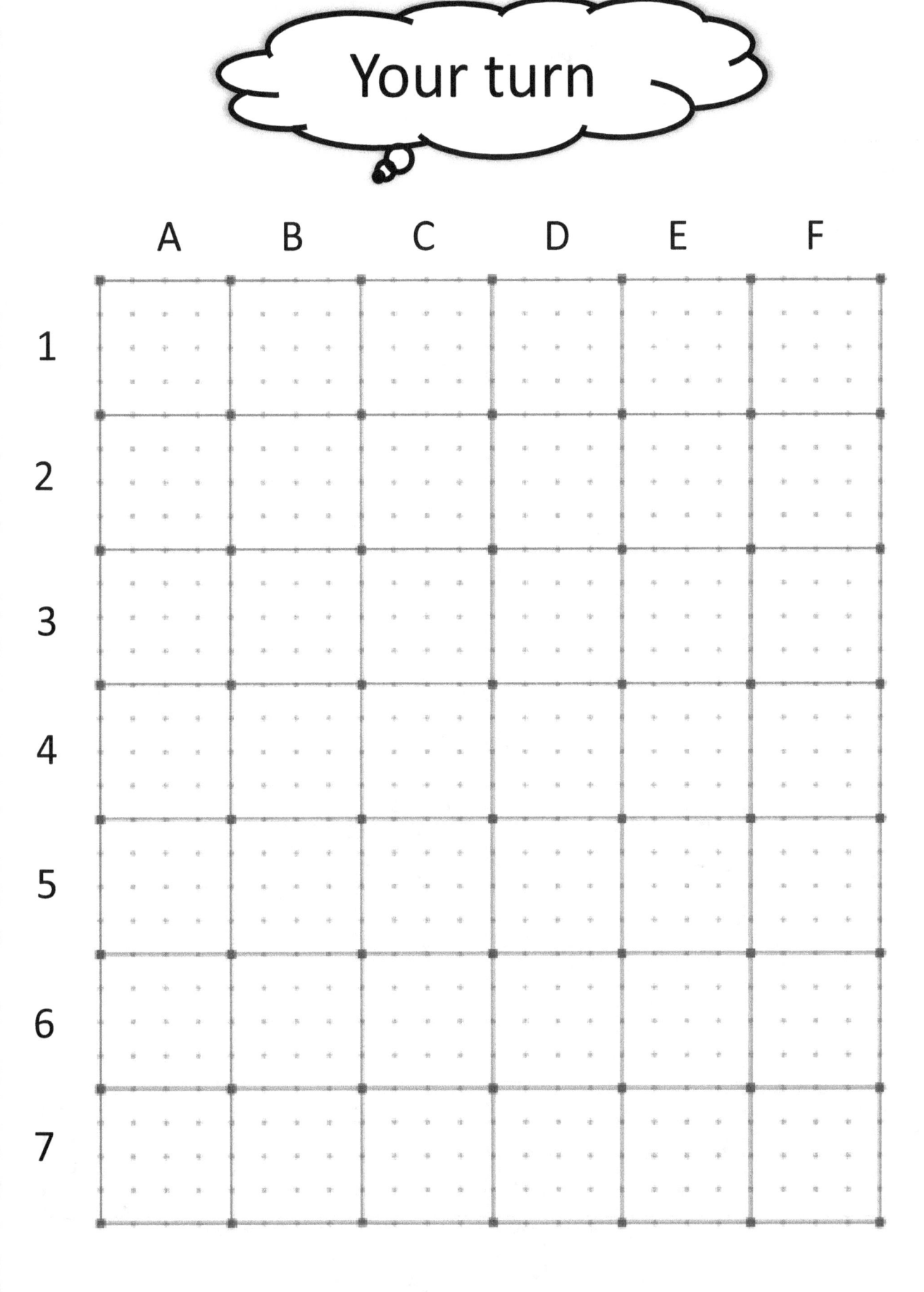

Trace It

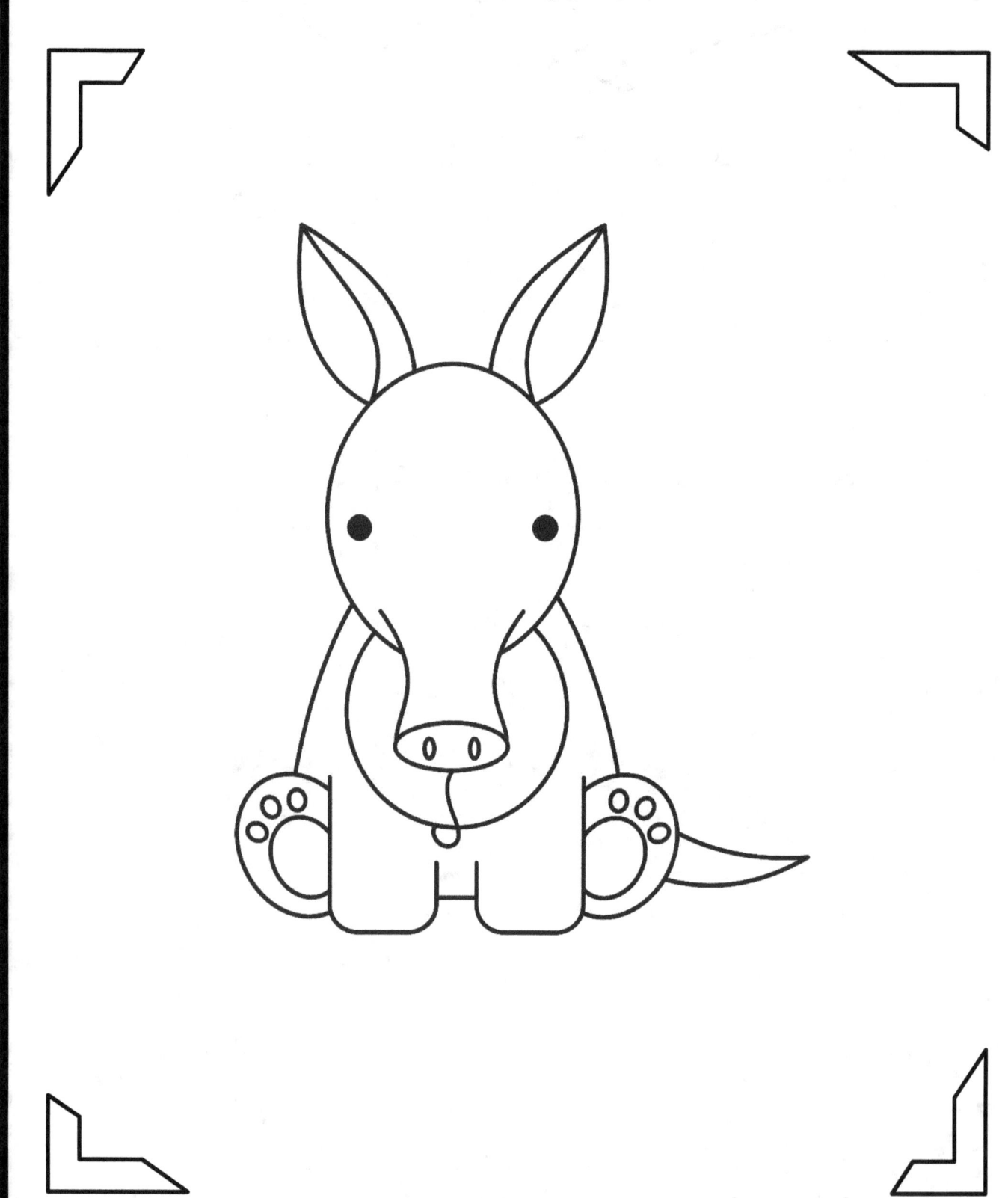

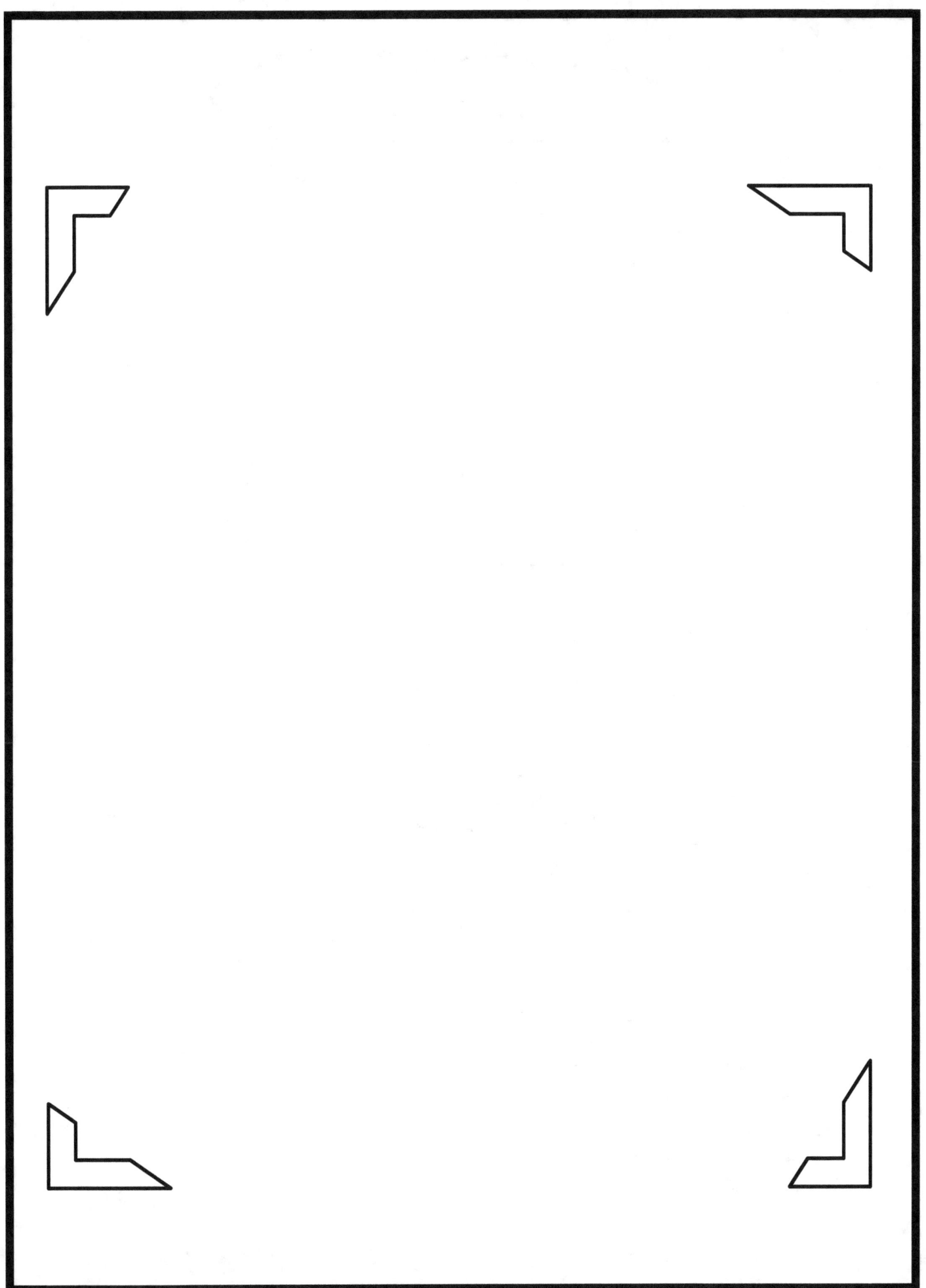

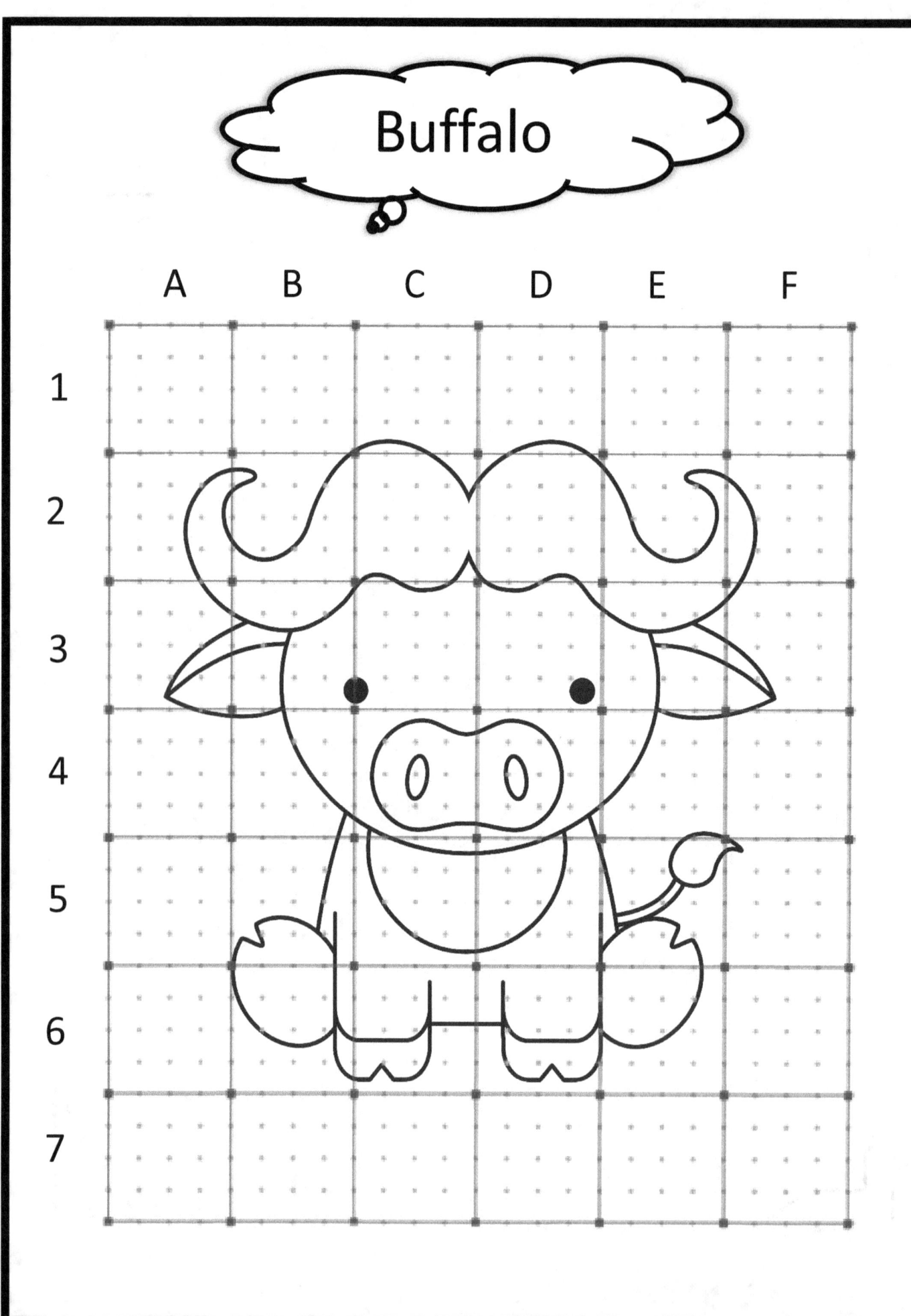

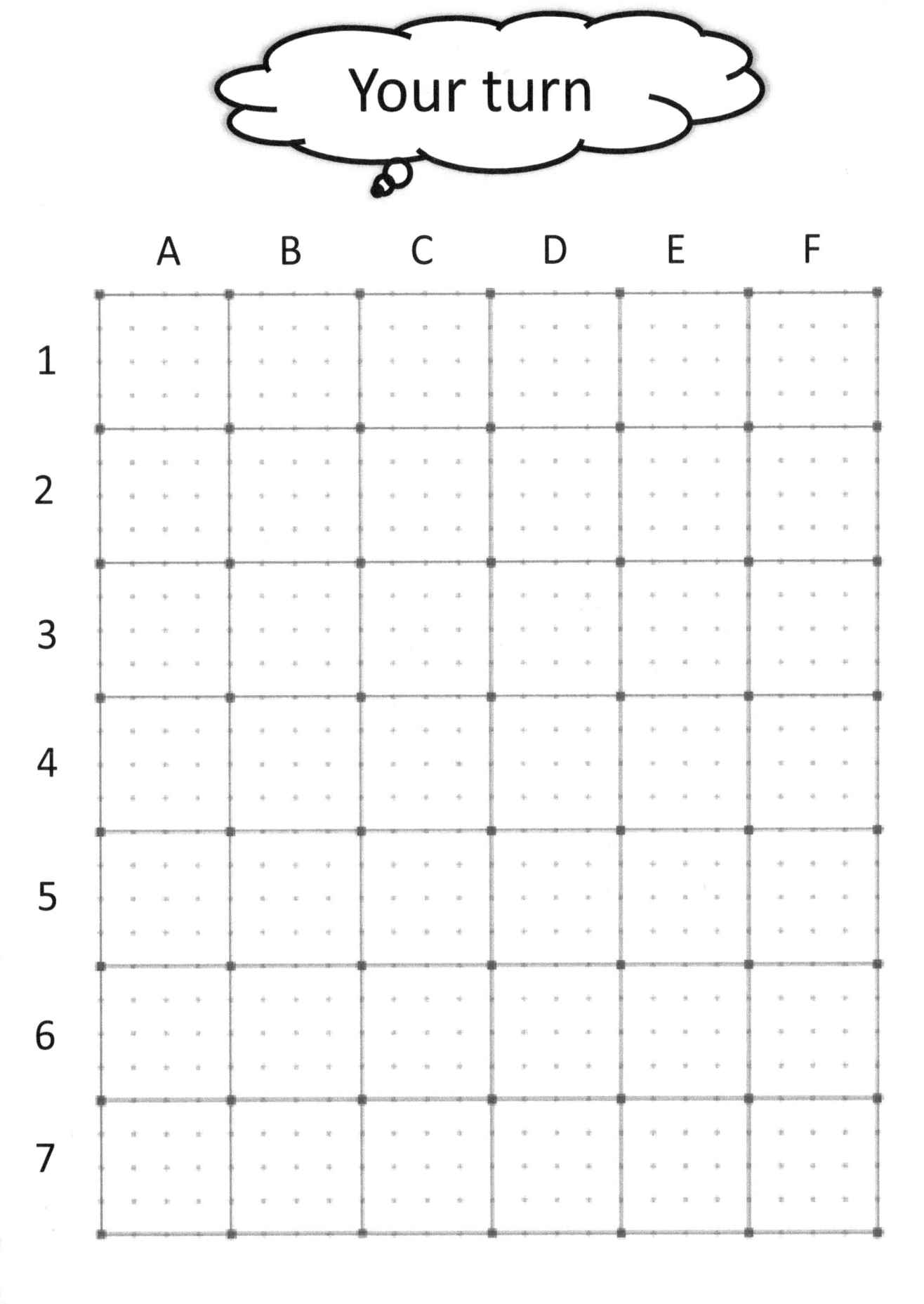

Trace It

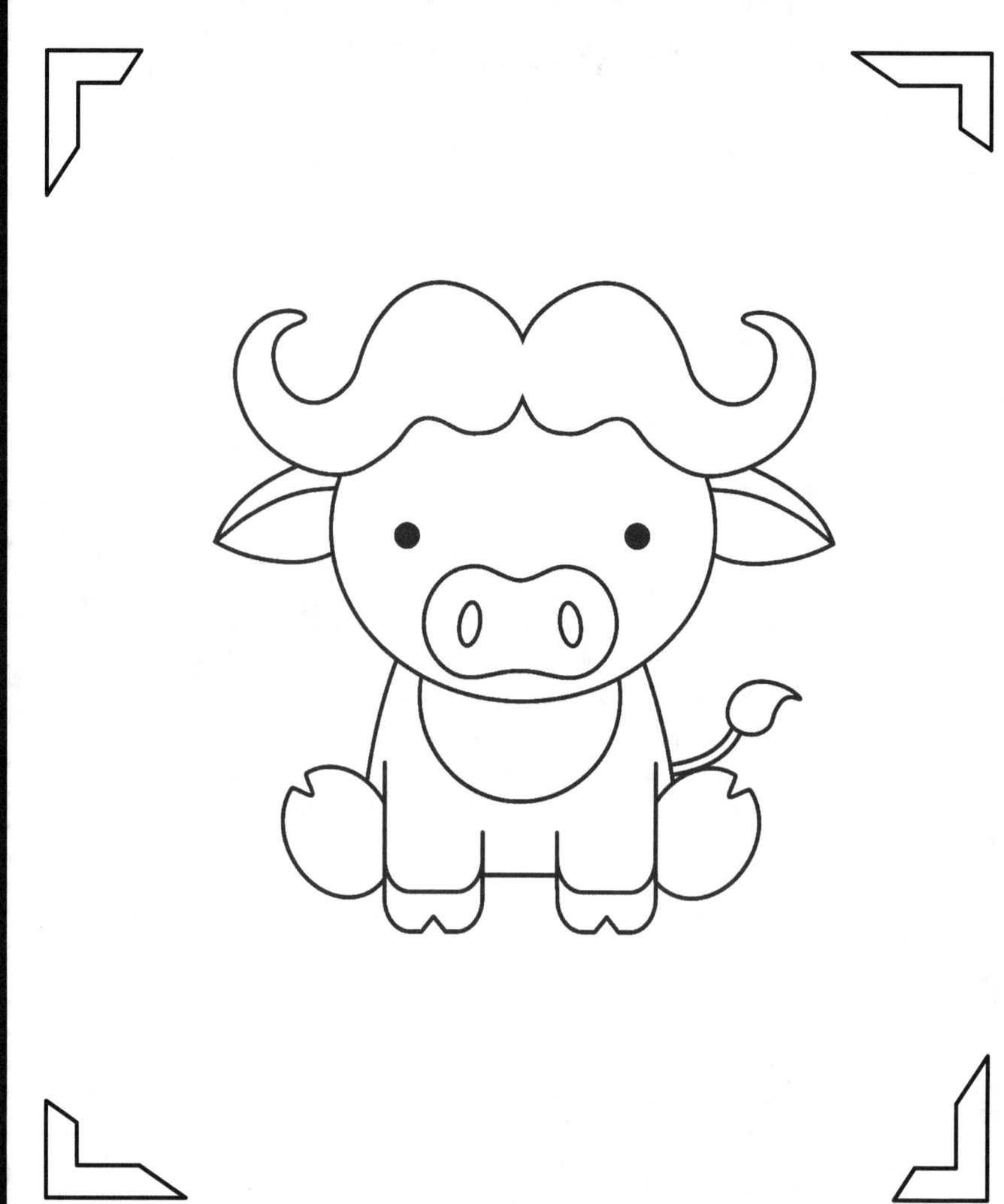

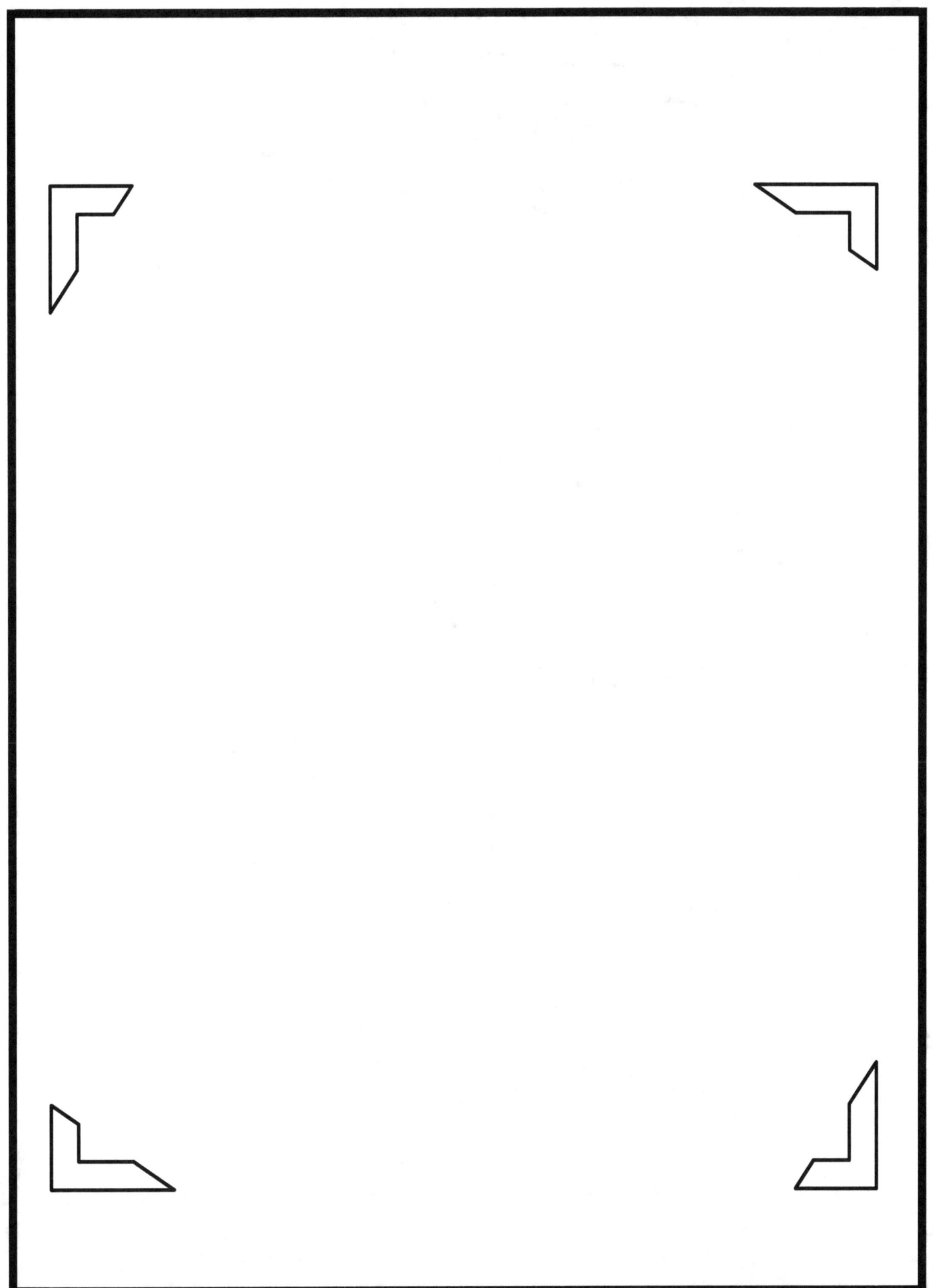

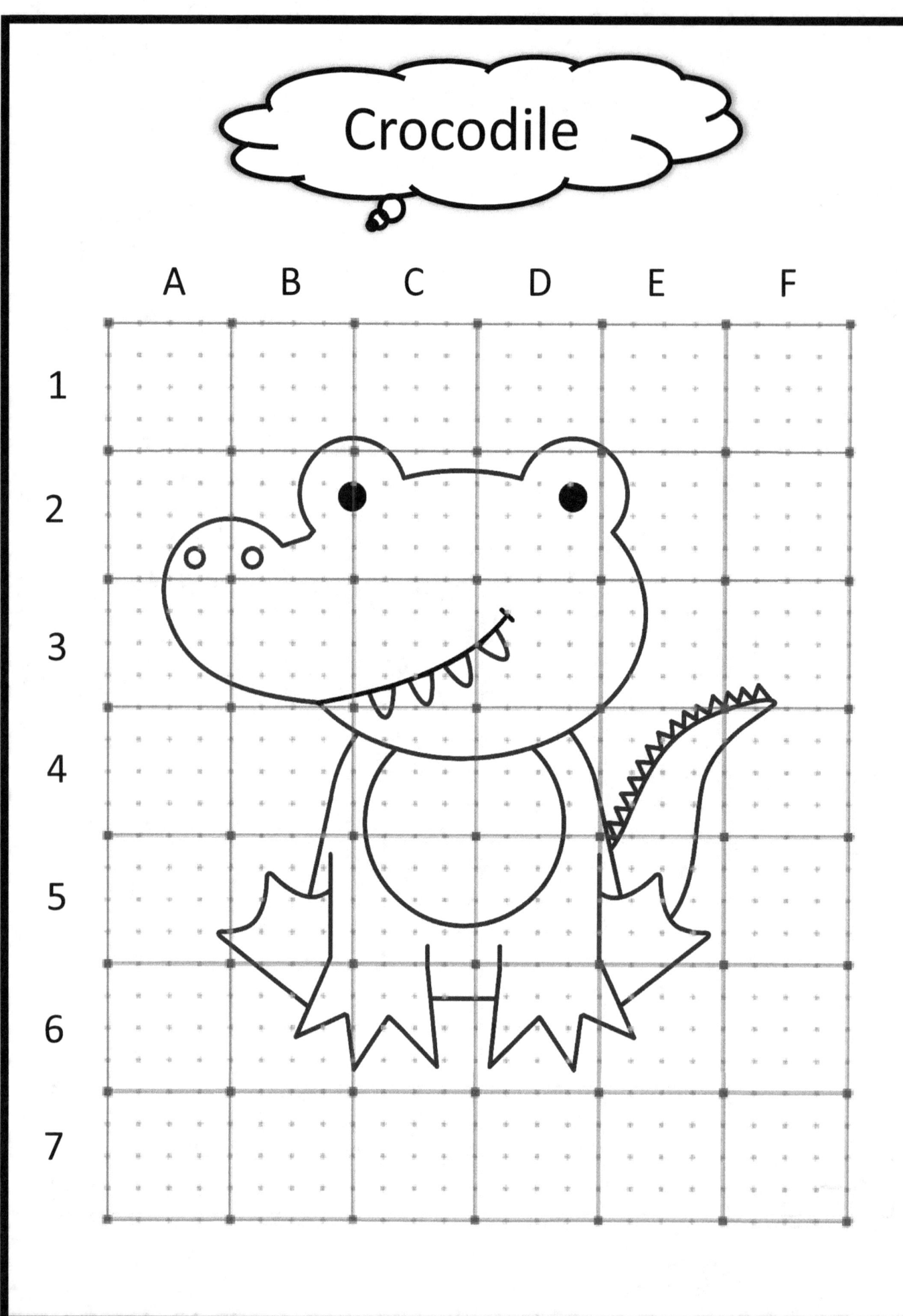

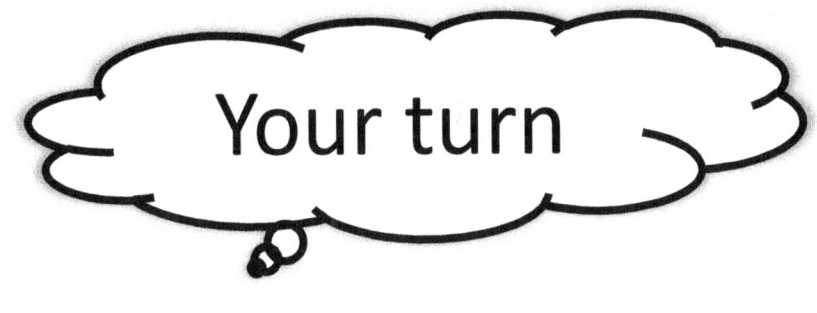

	A	B	C	D	E	F
1						
2						
3						
4						
5						
6						
7						

Trace It

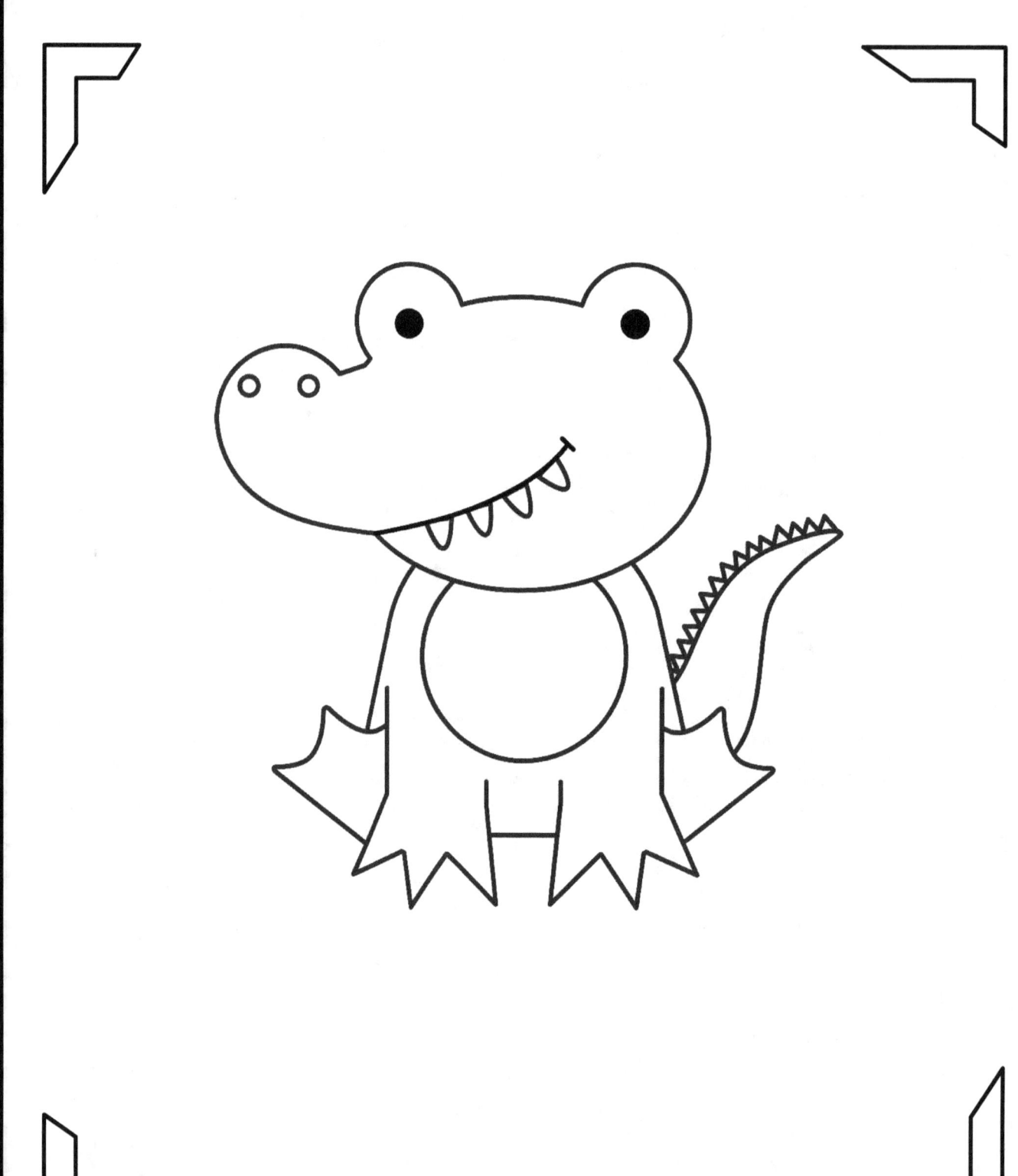

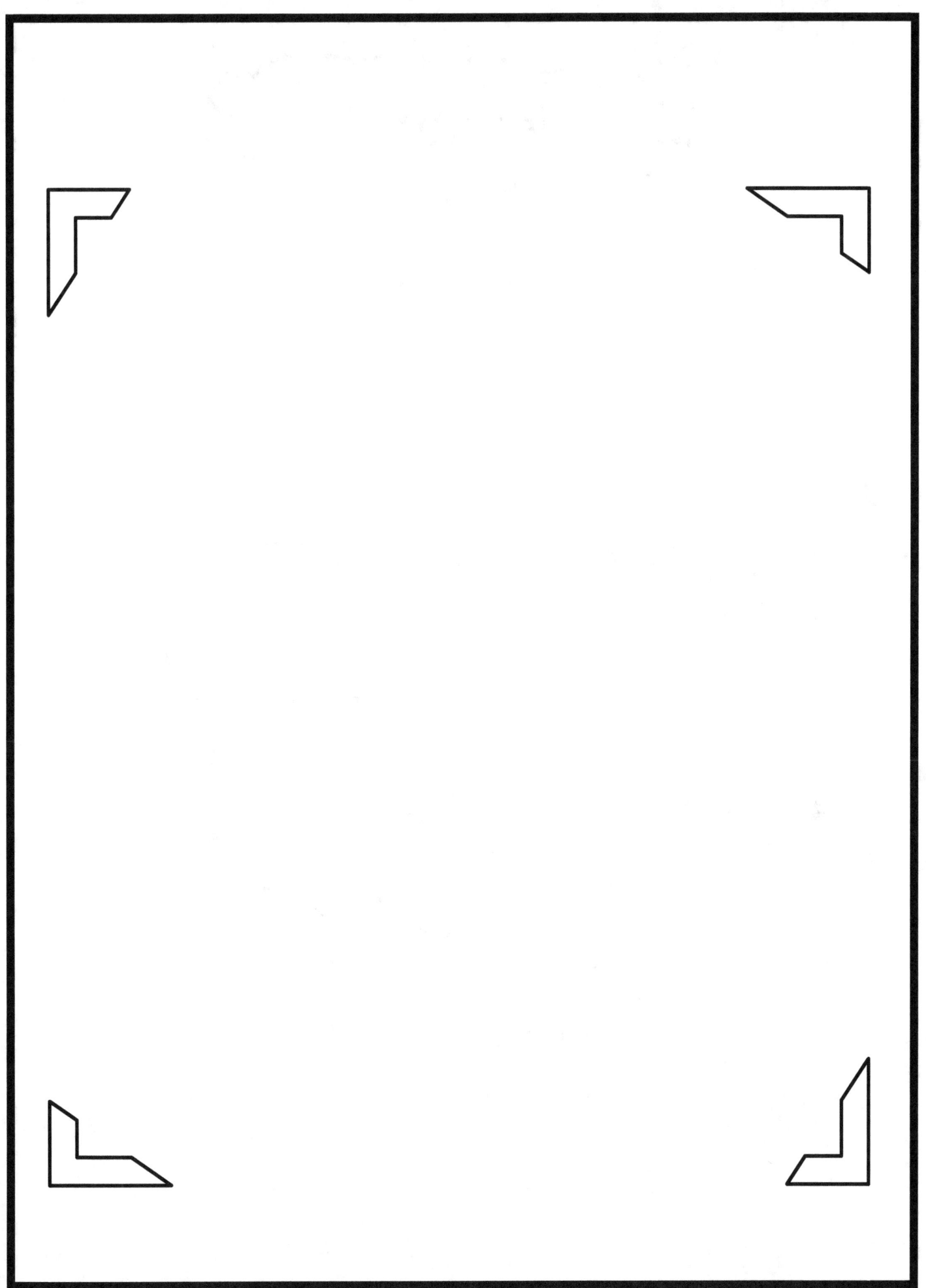

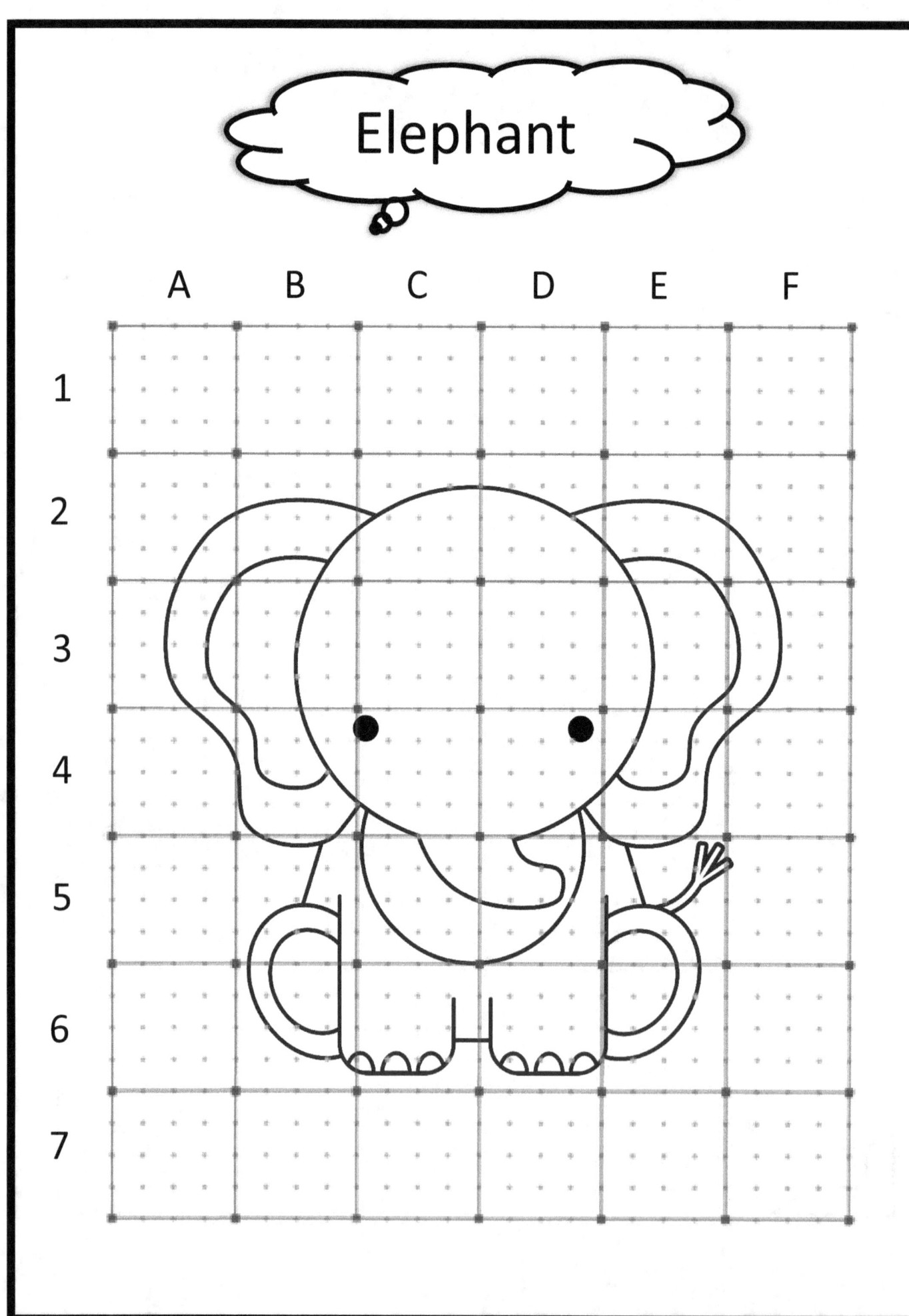

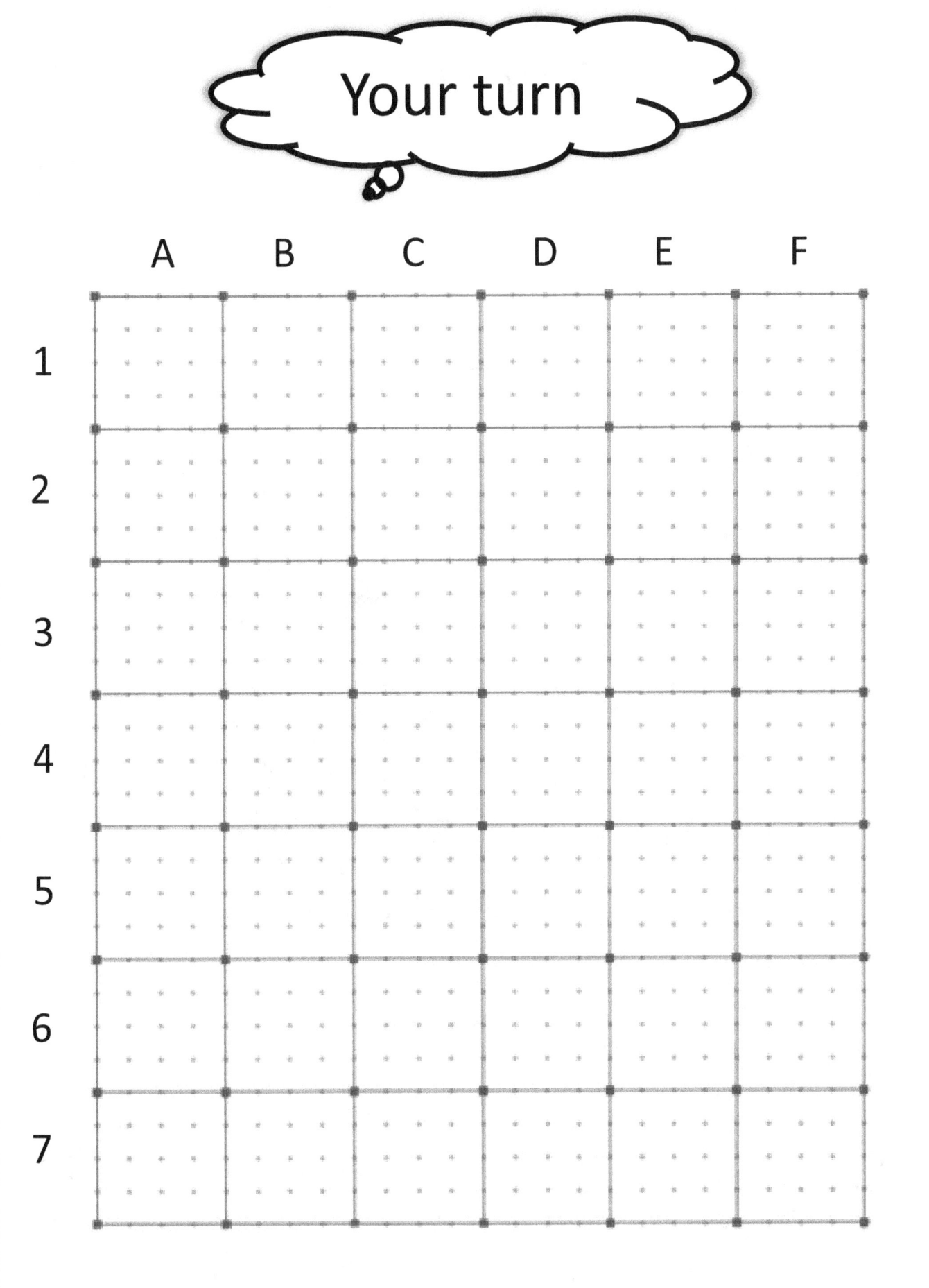

Trace It

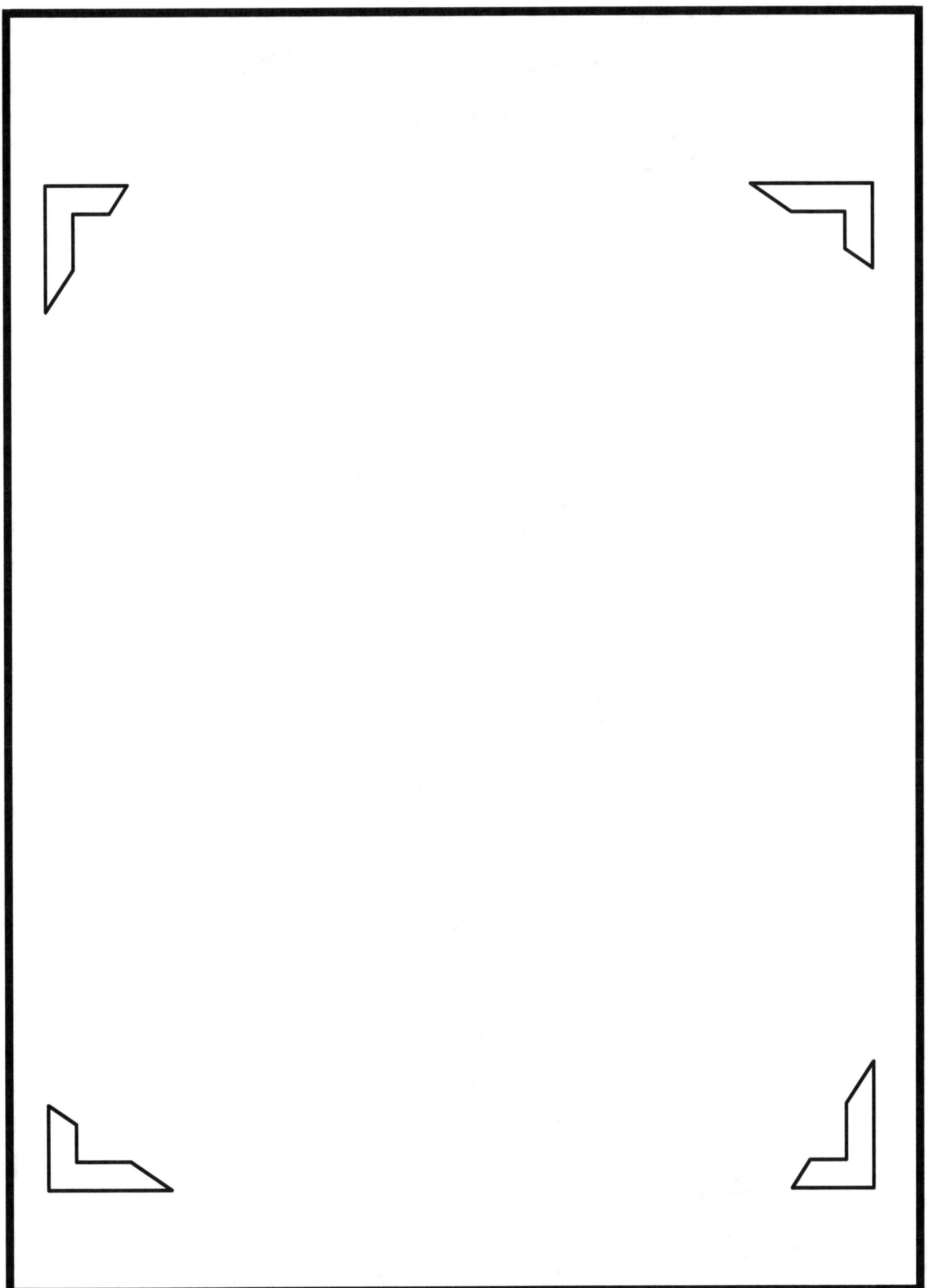

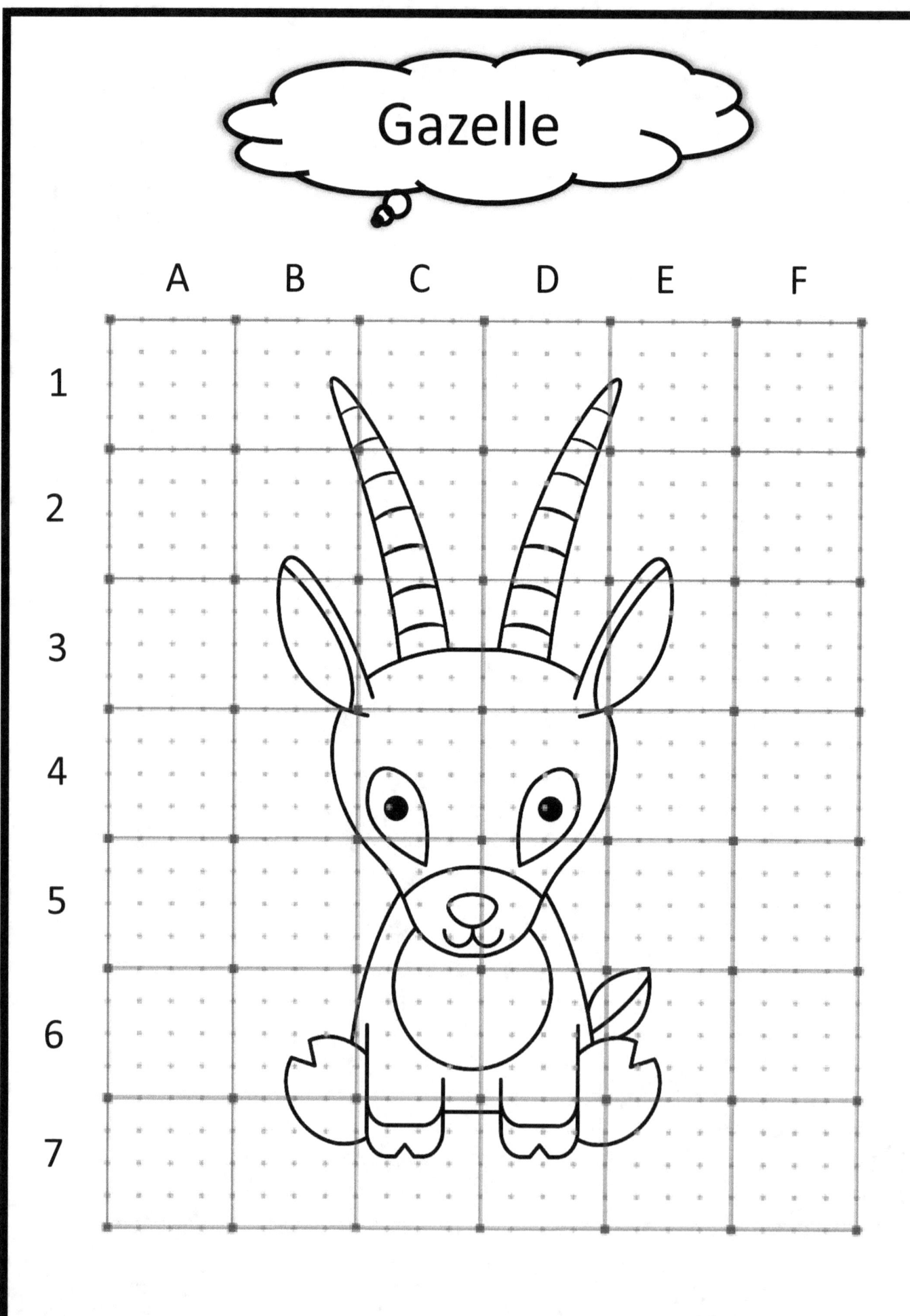

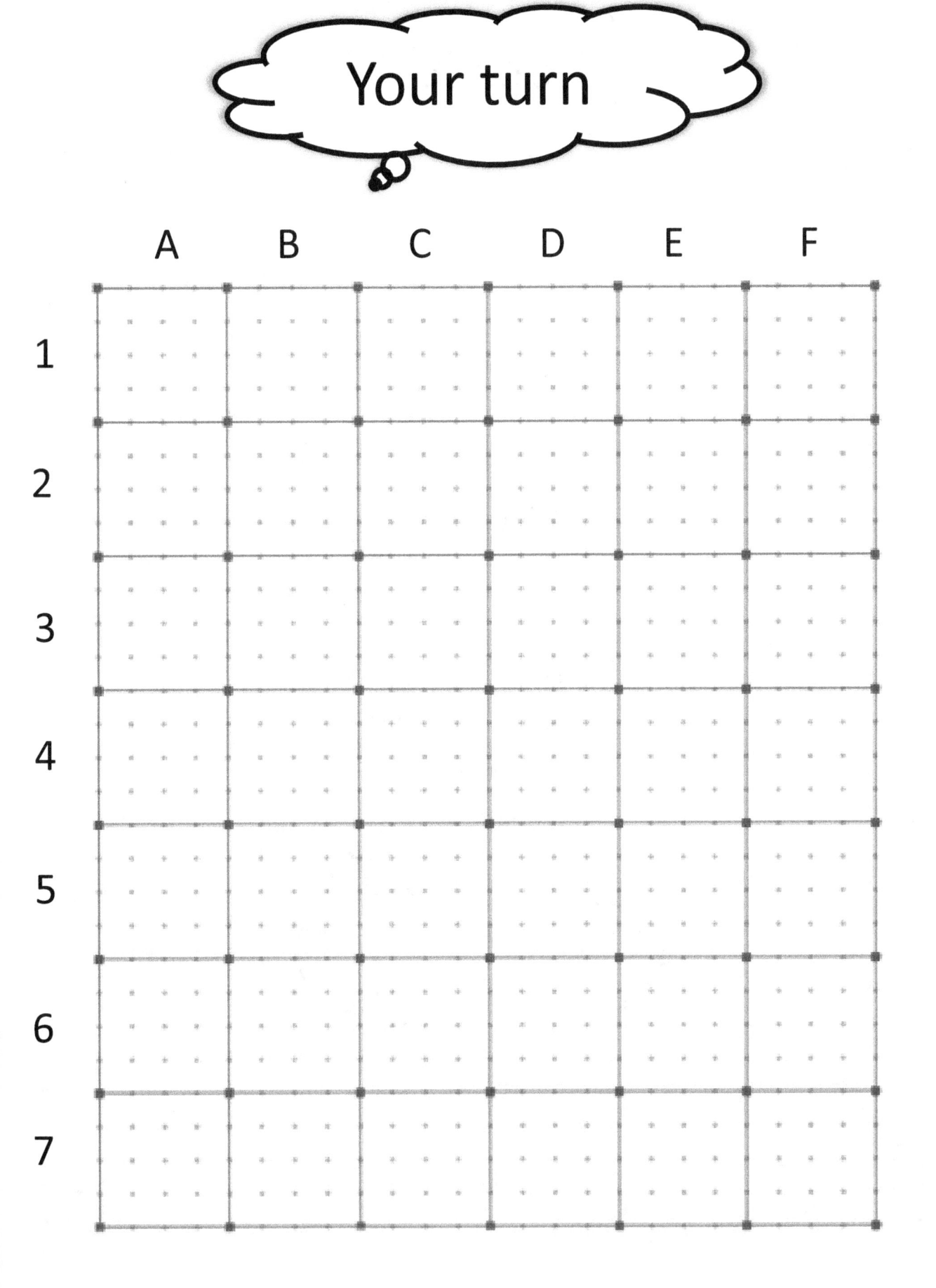

Trace It

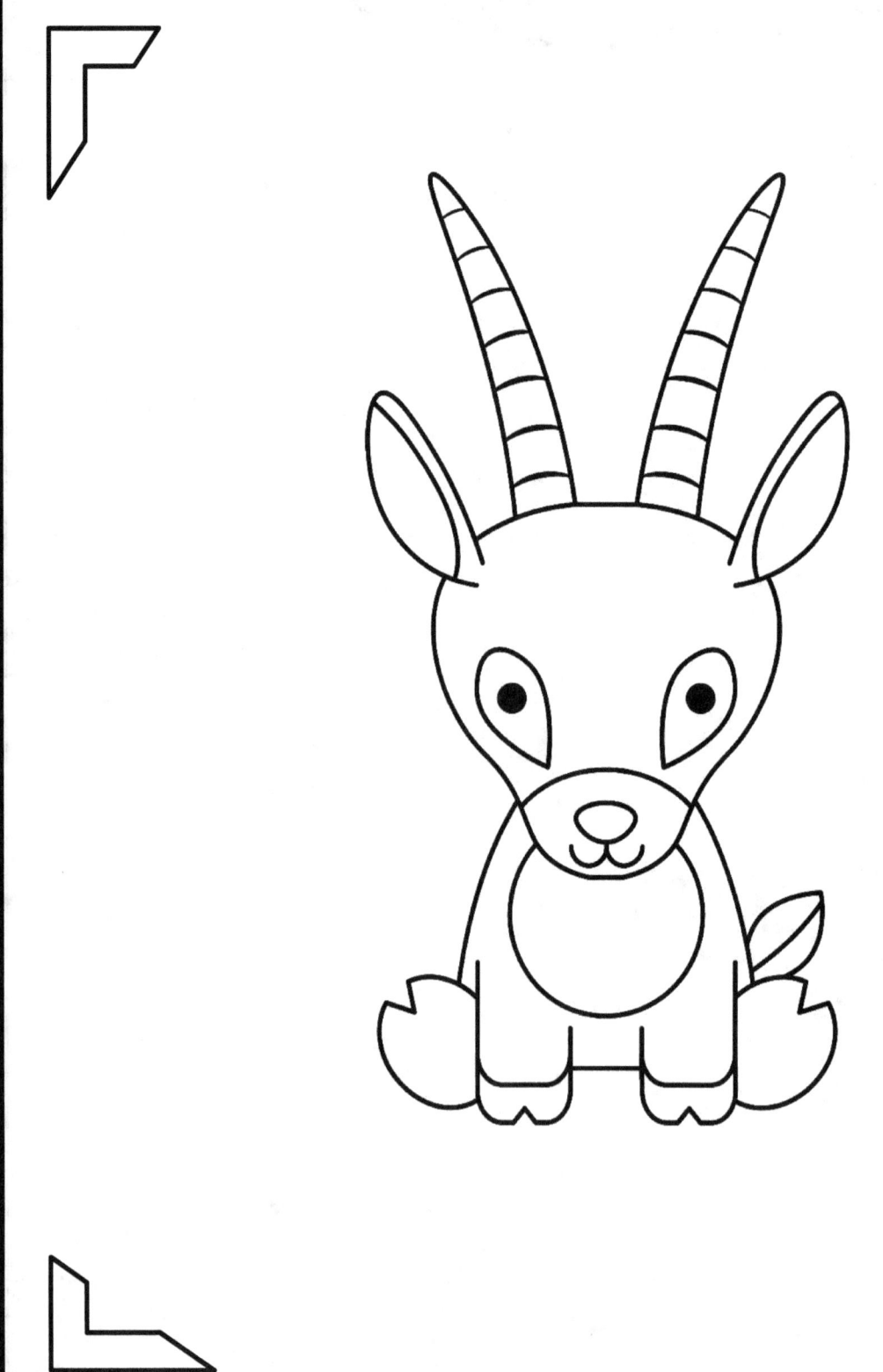

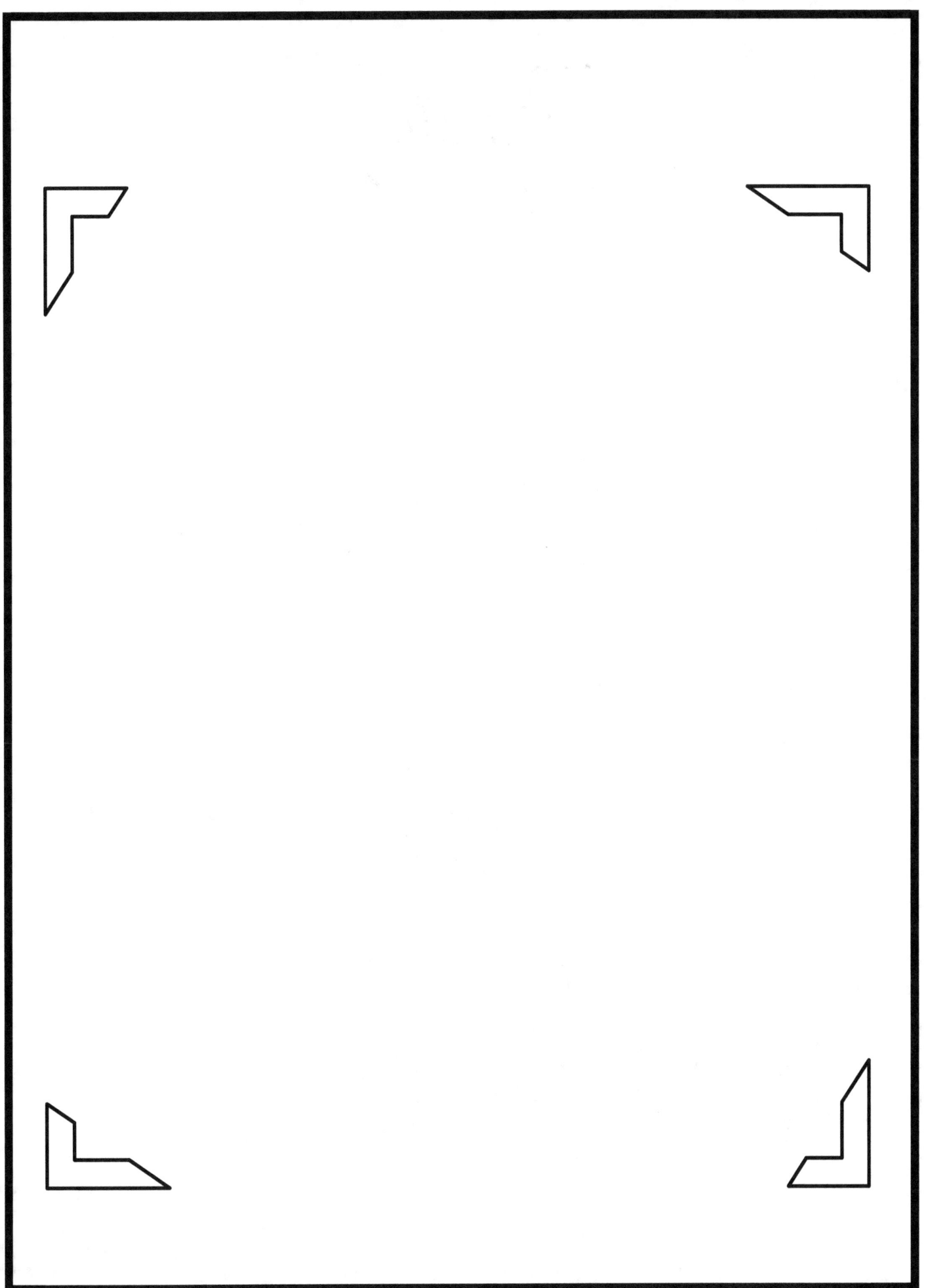

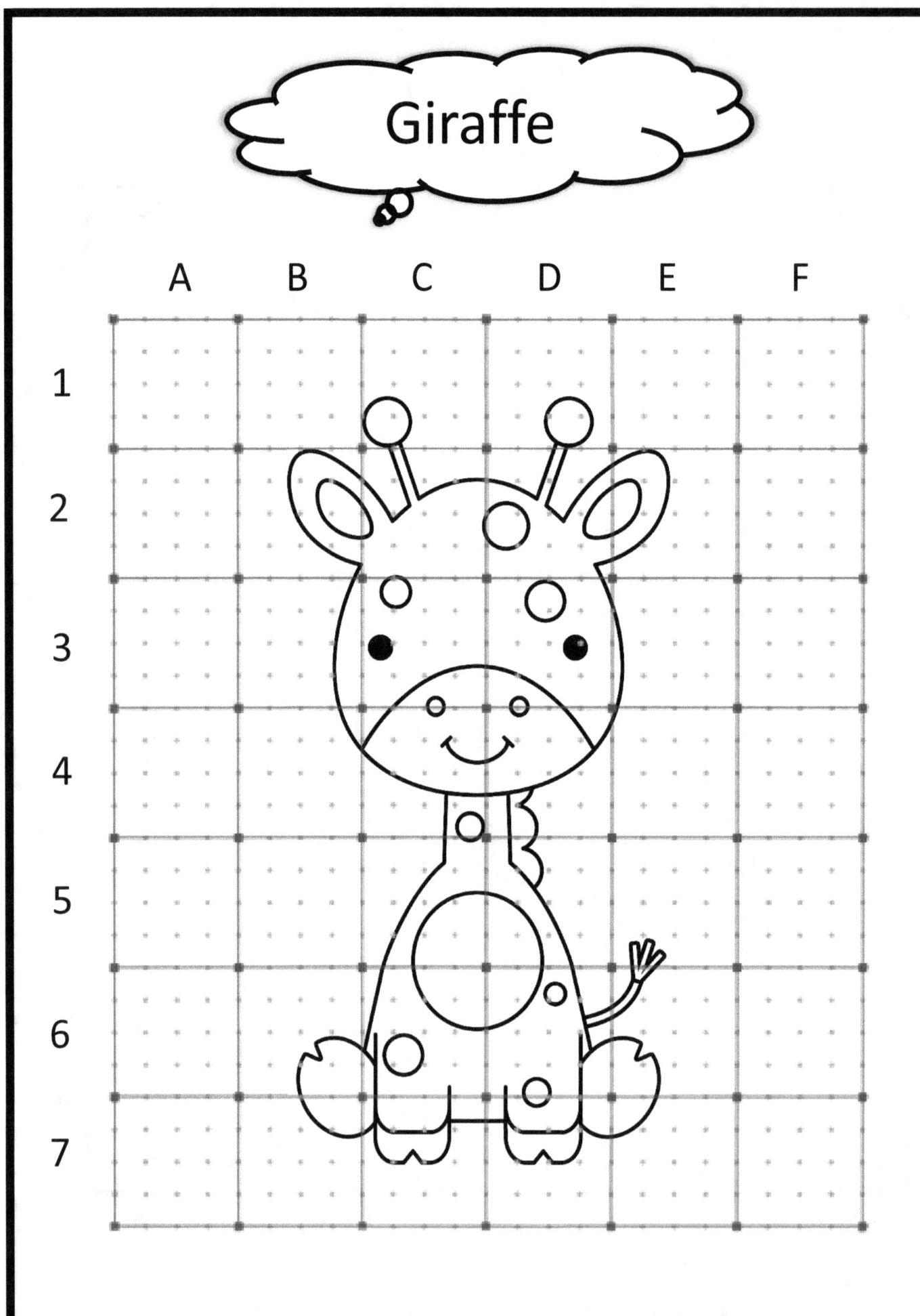

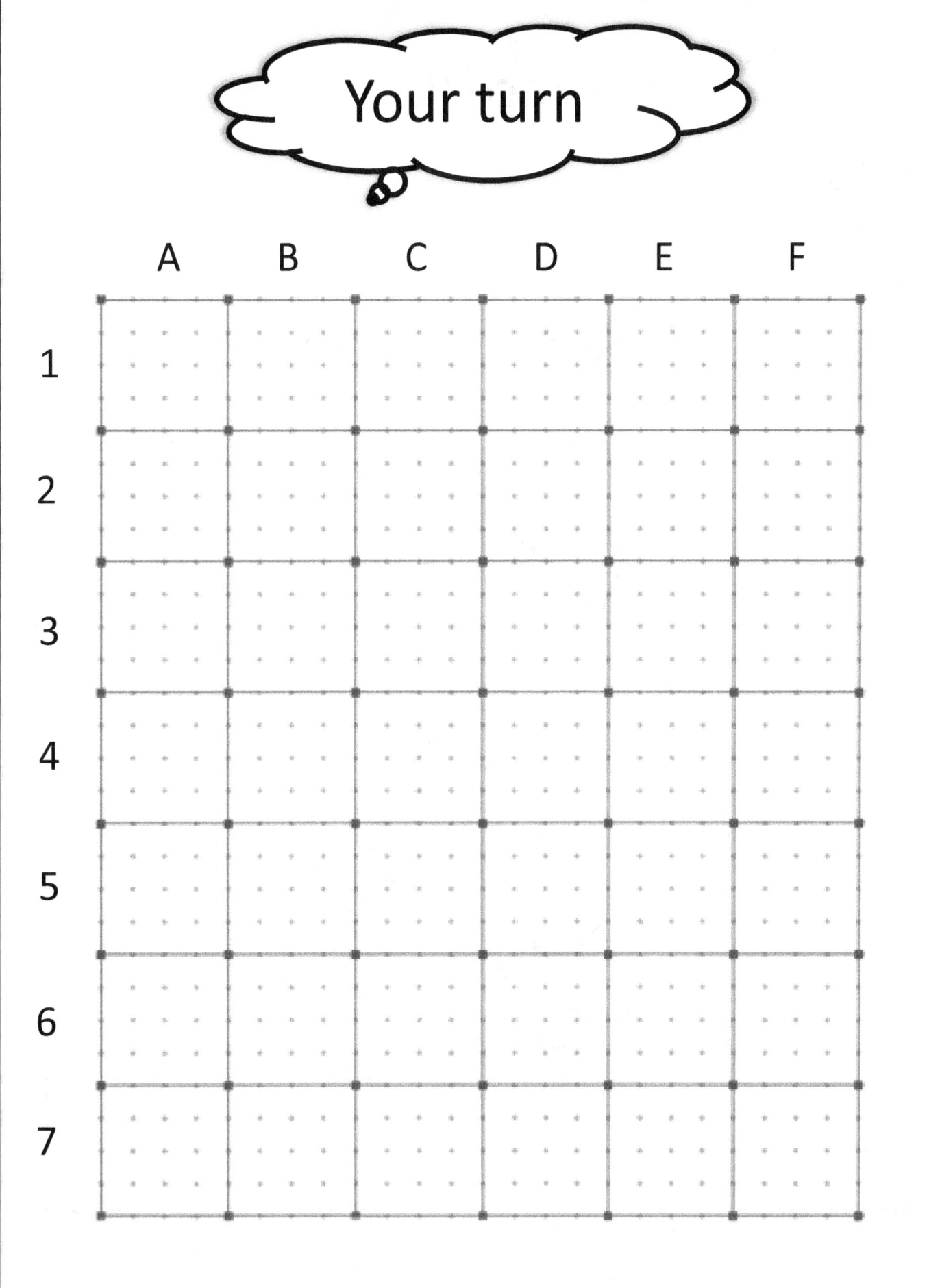

Trace It

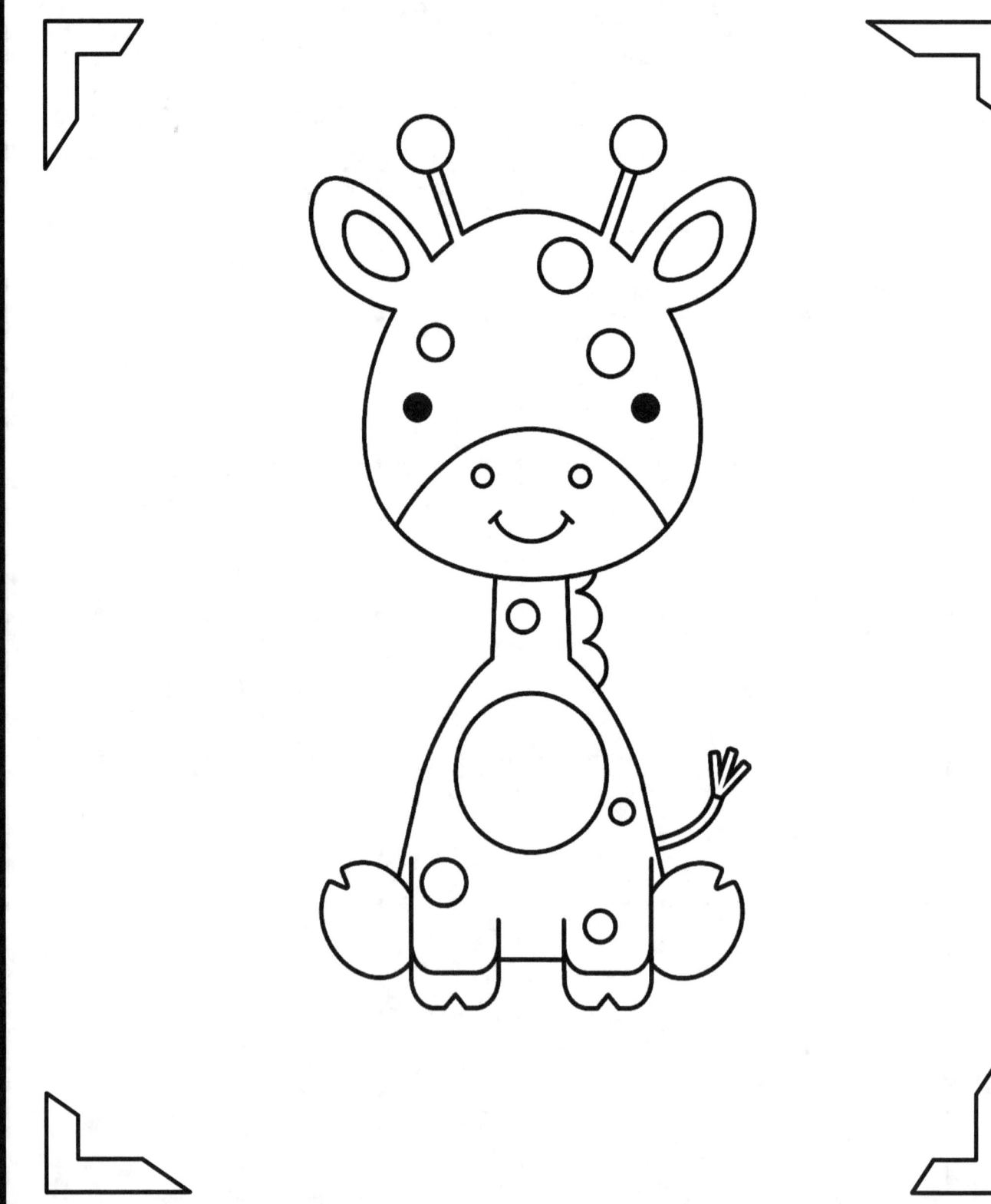

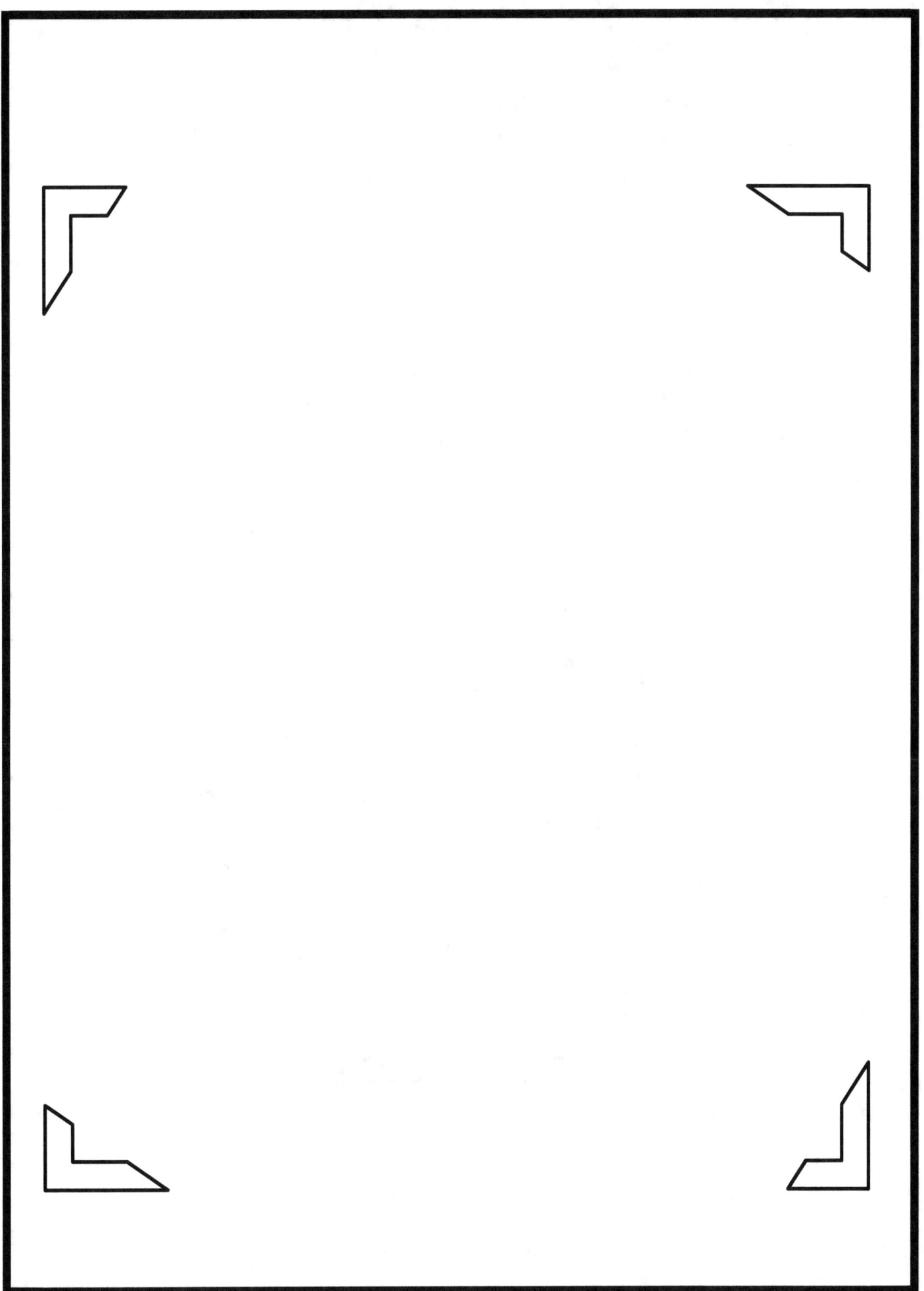

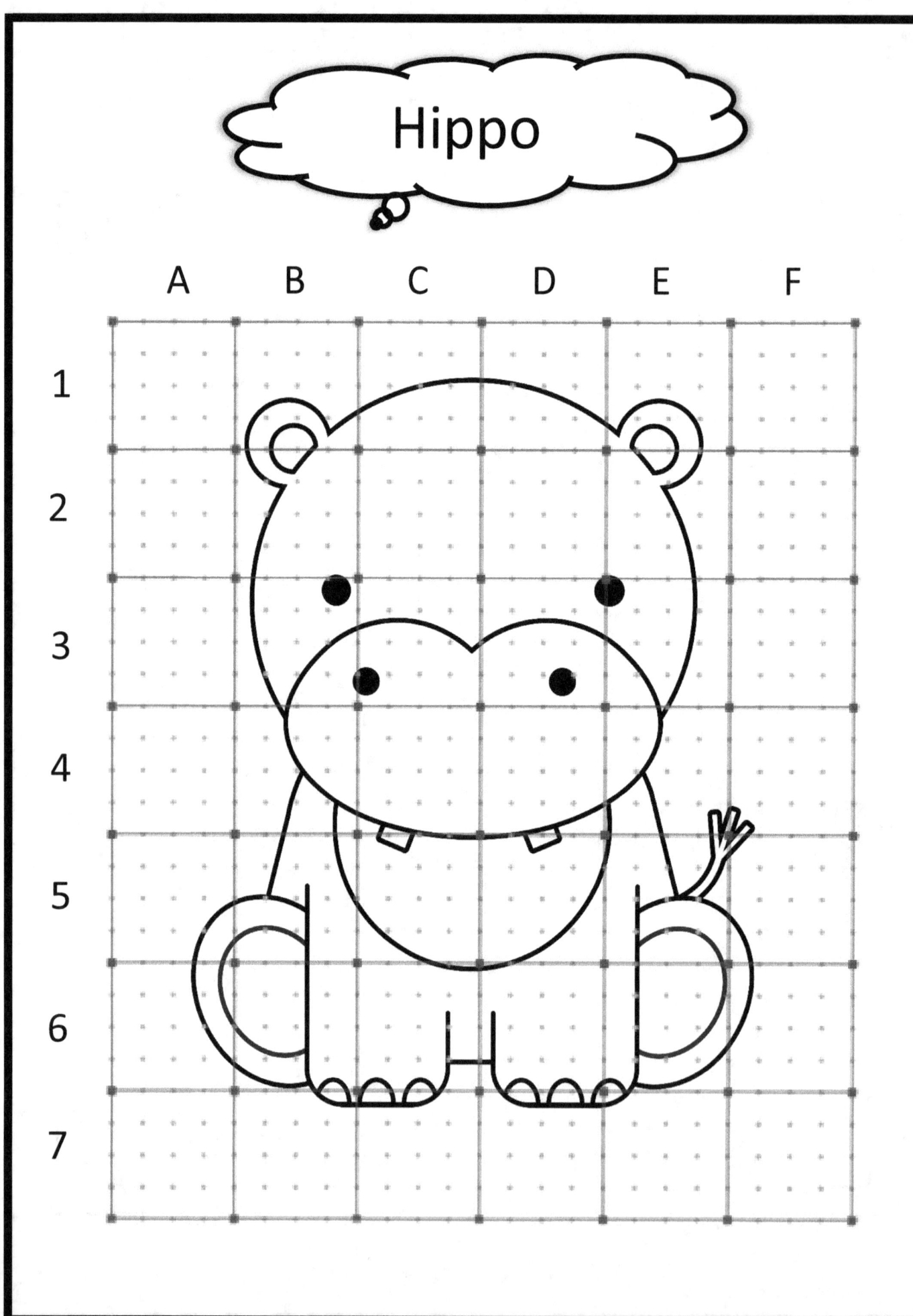

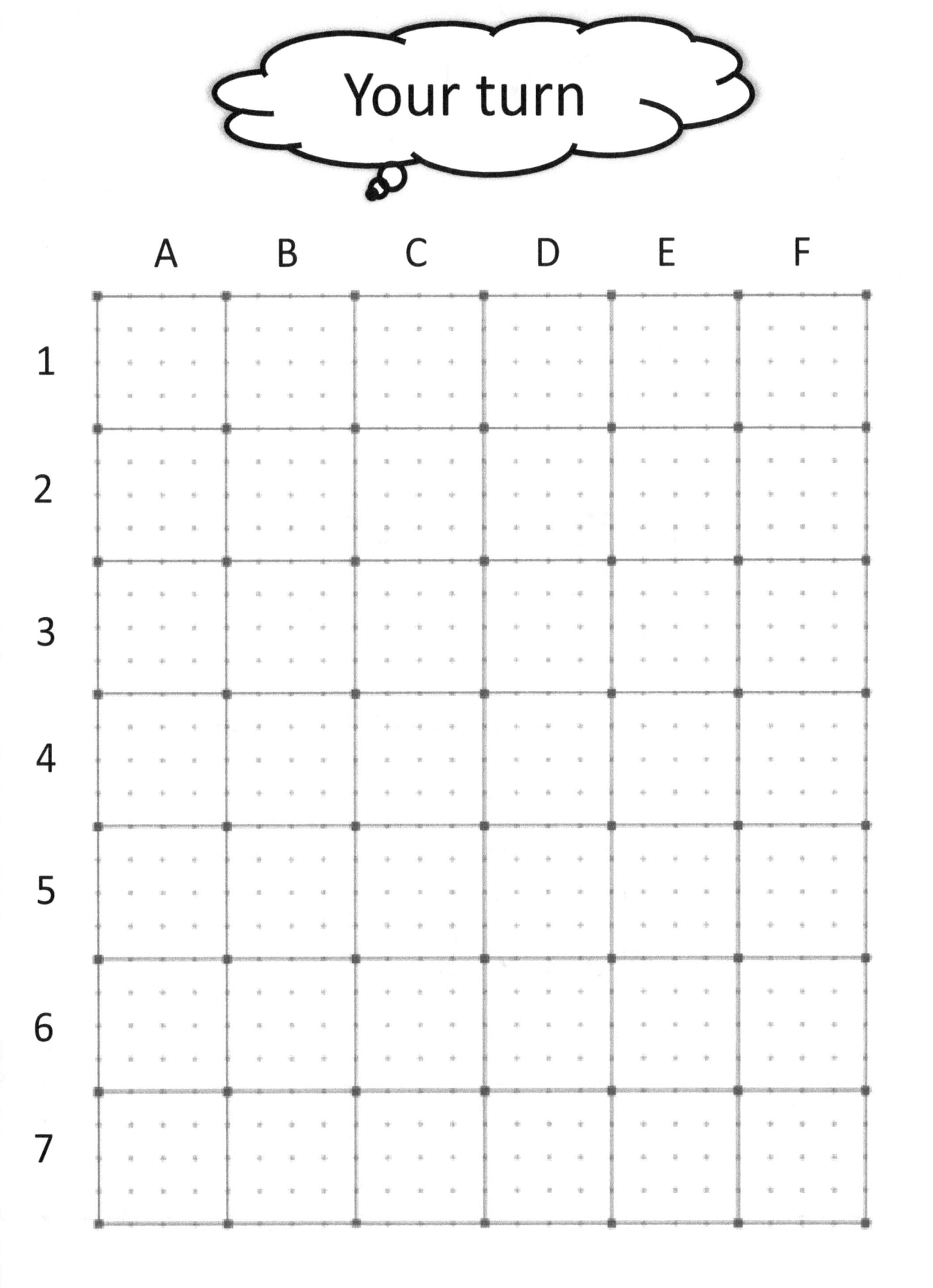

Trace It

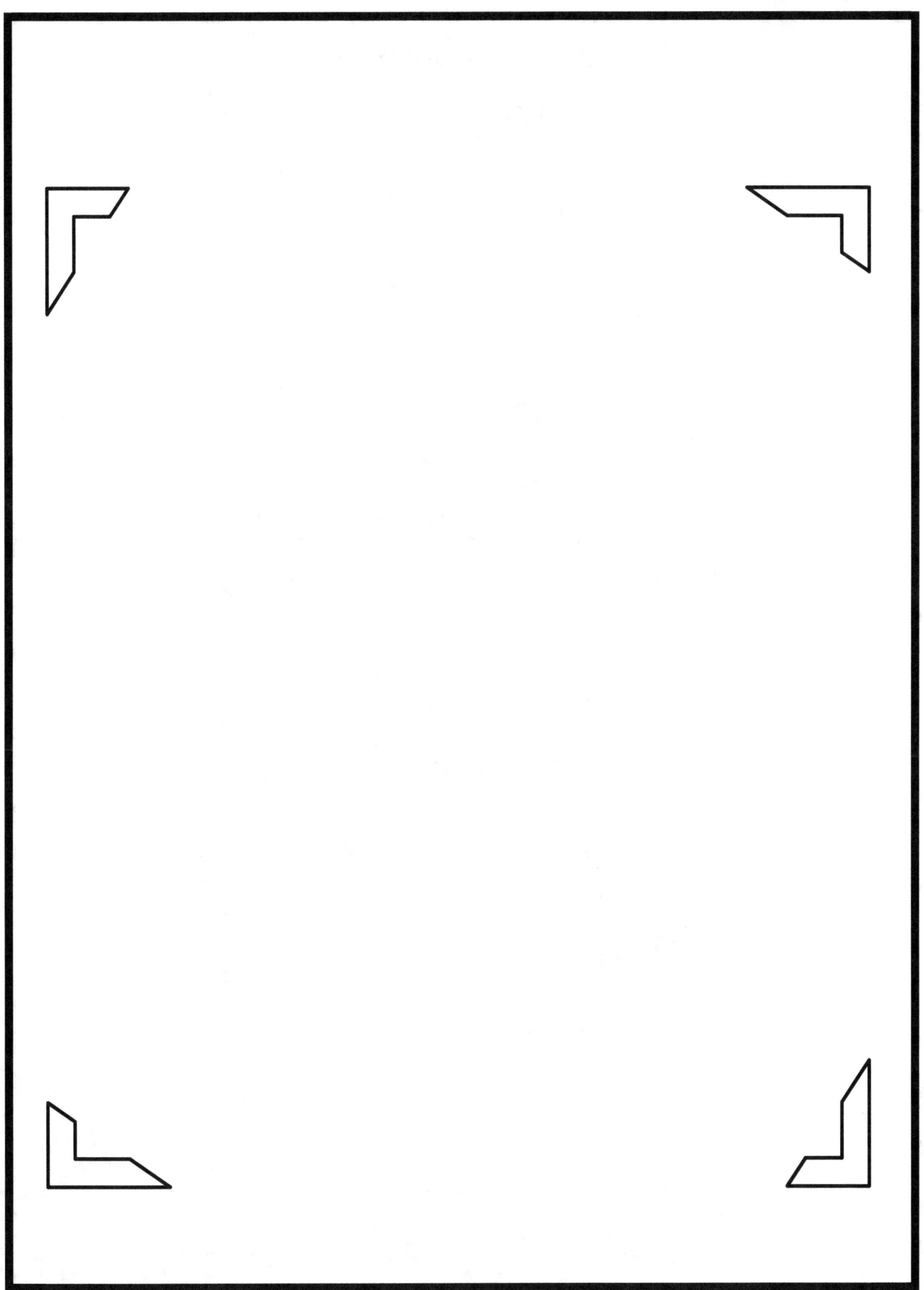

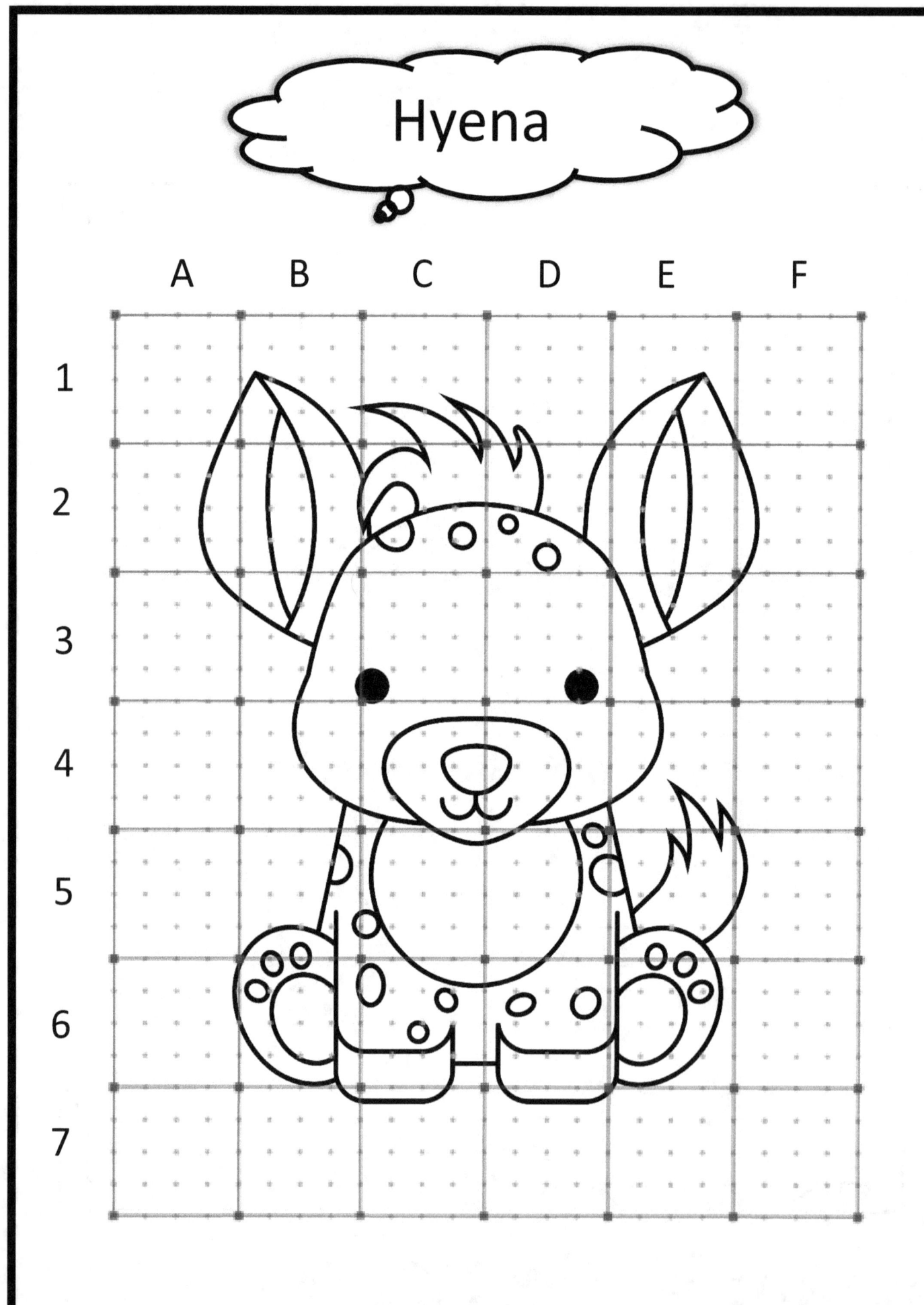

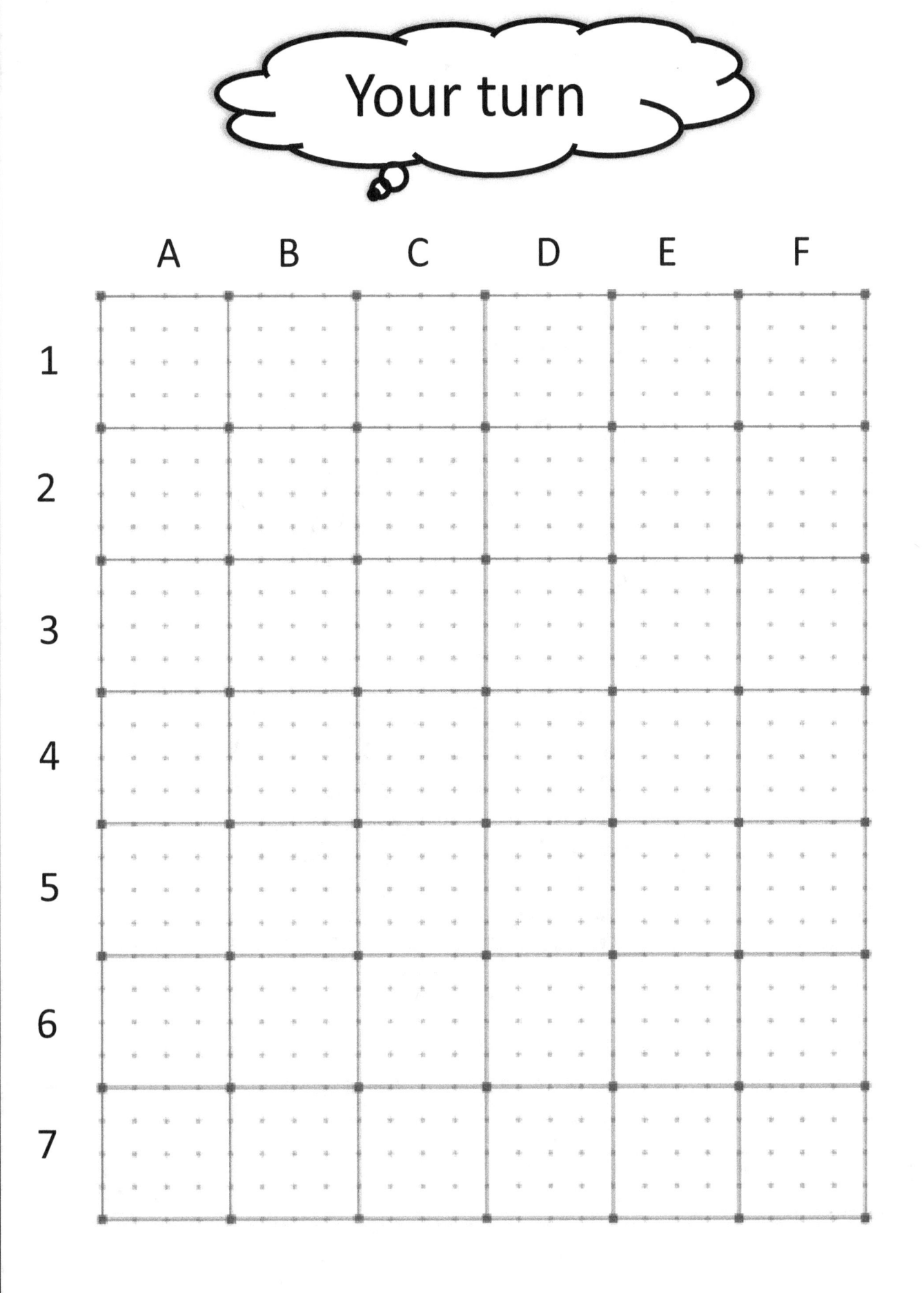

Trace It

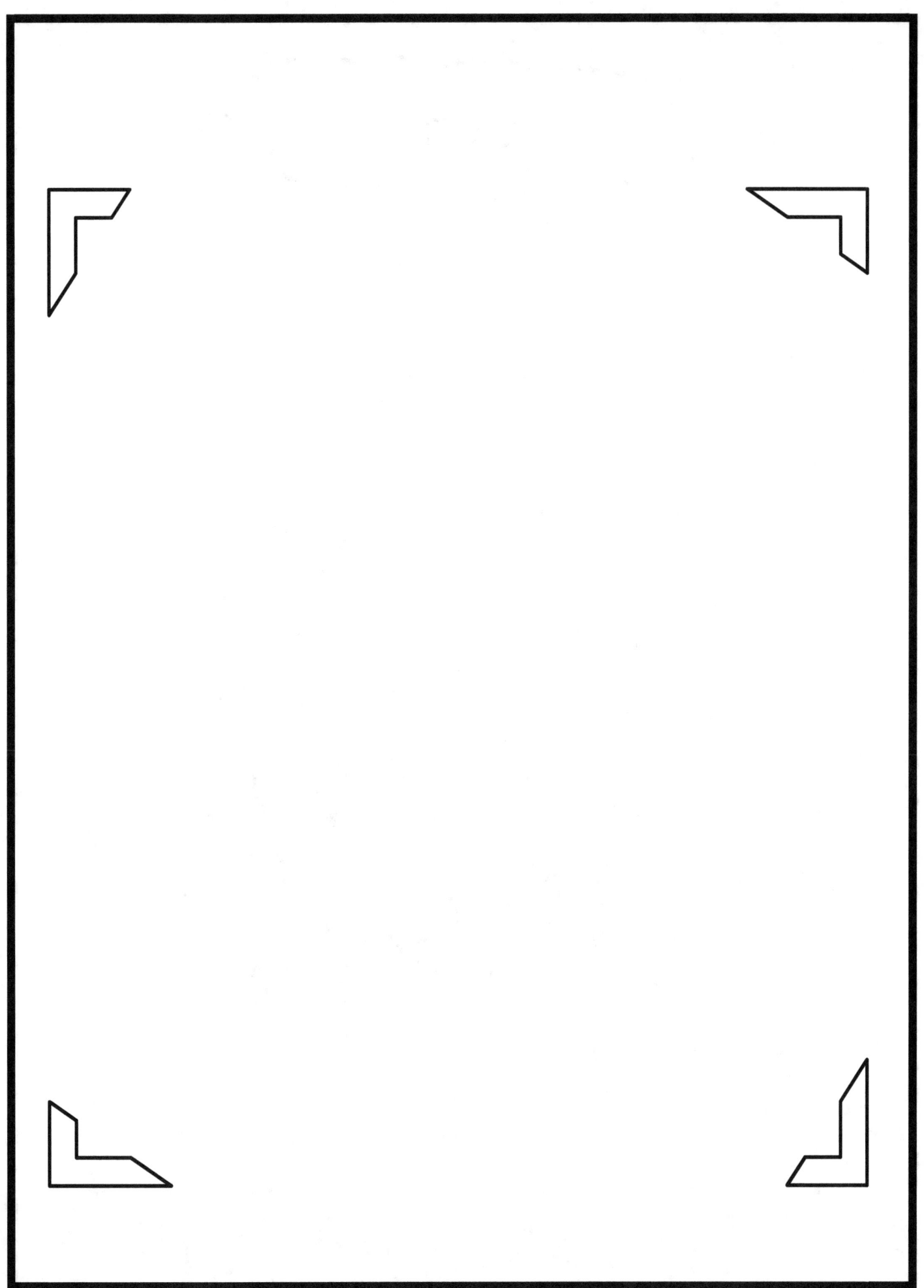

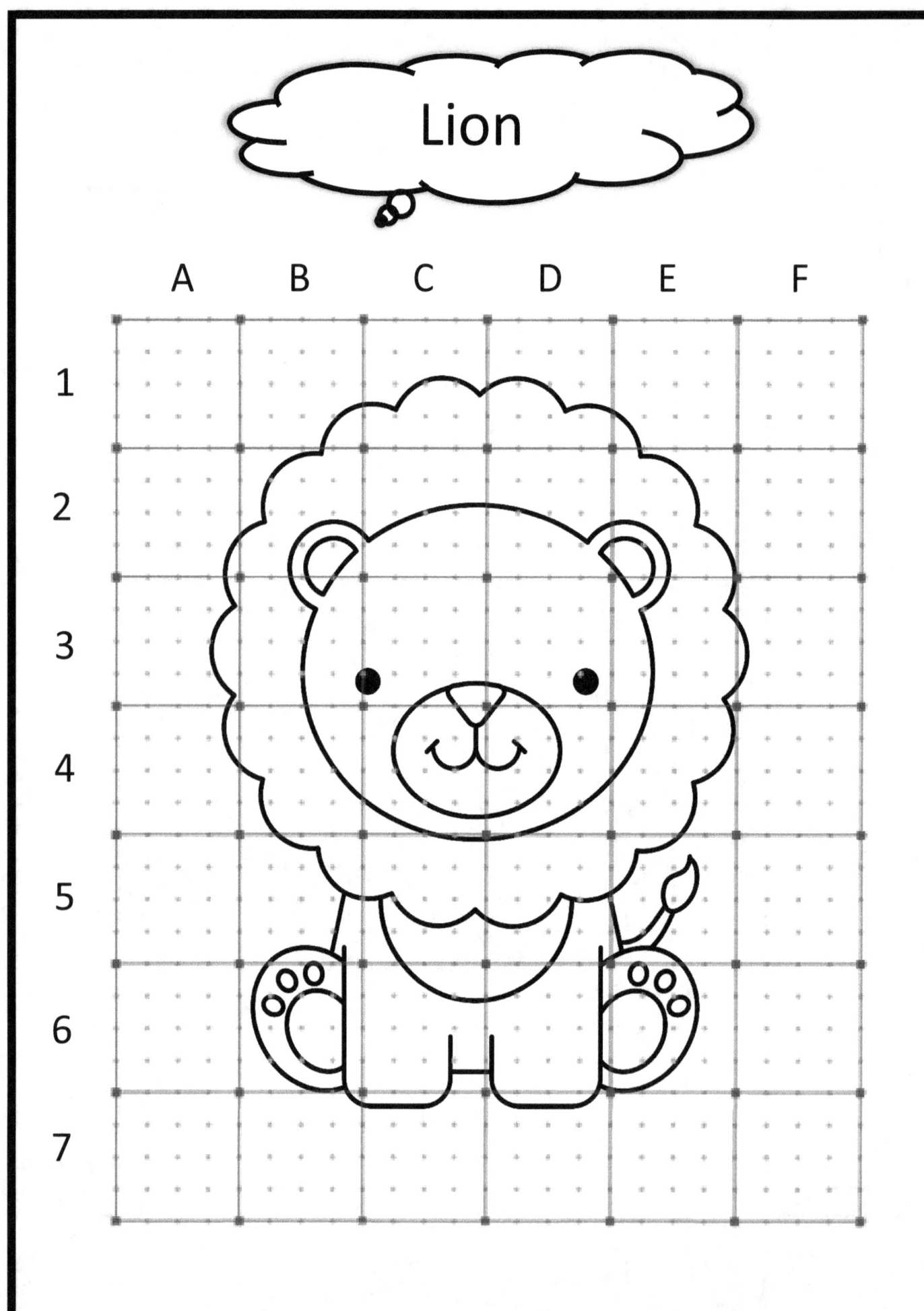

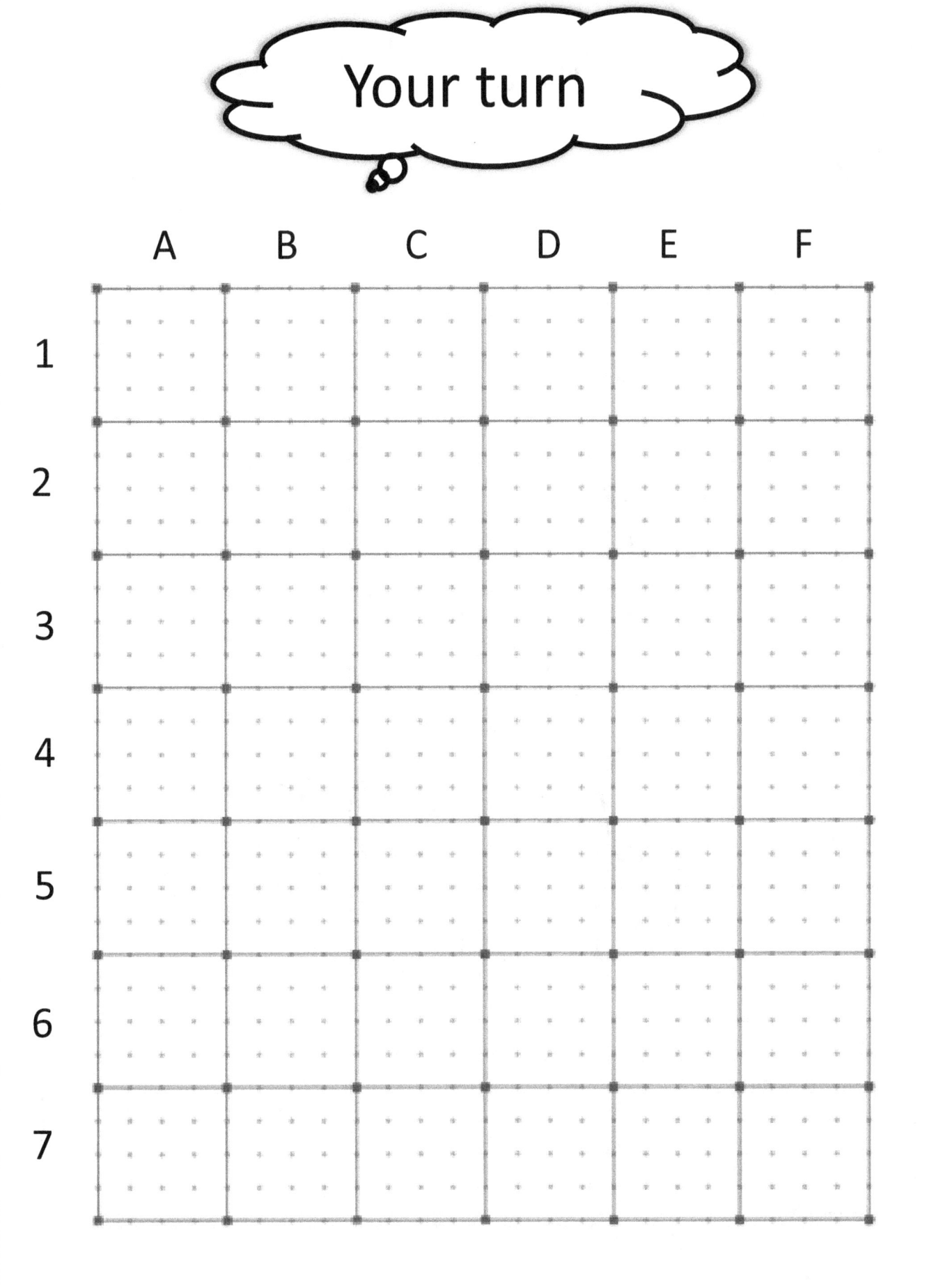

Trace It

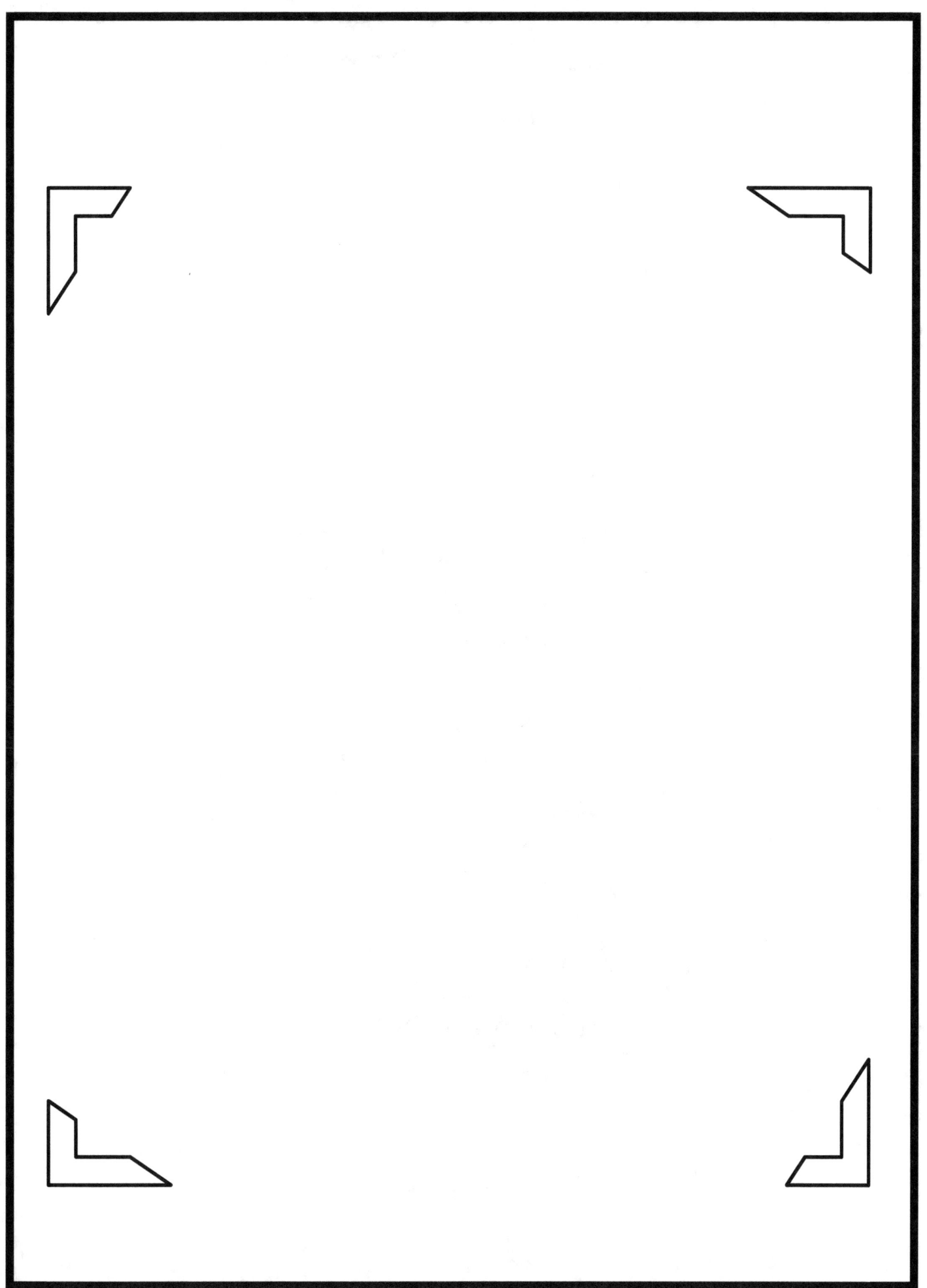

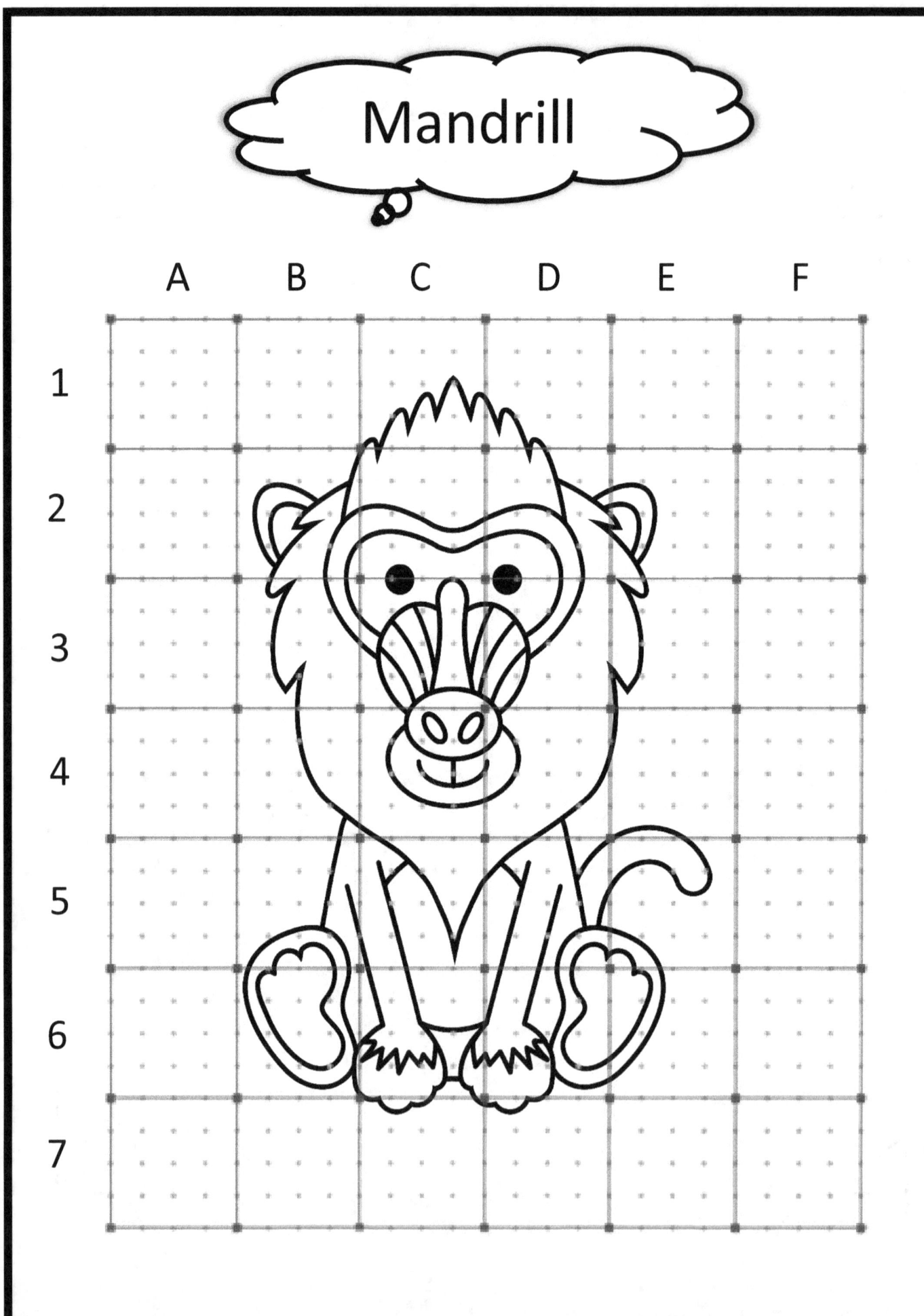

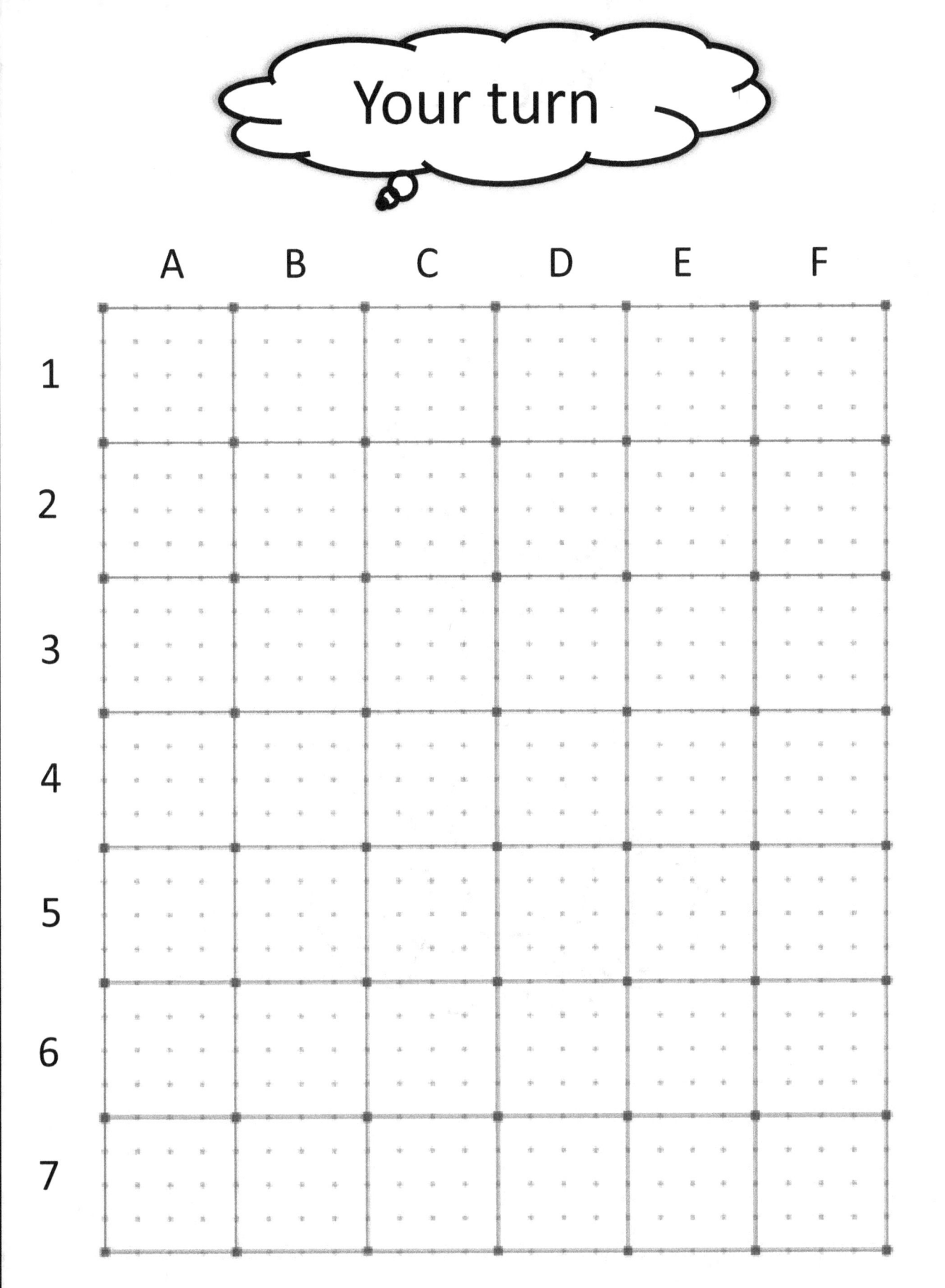

Trace It

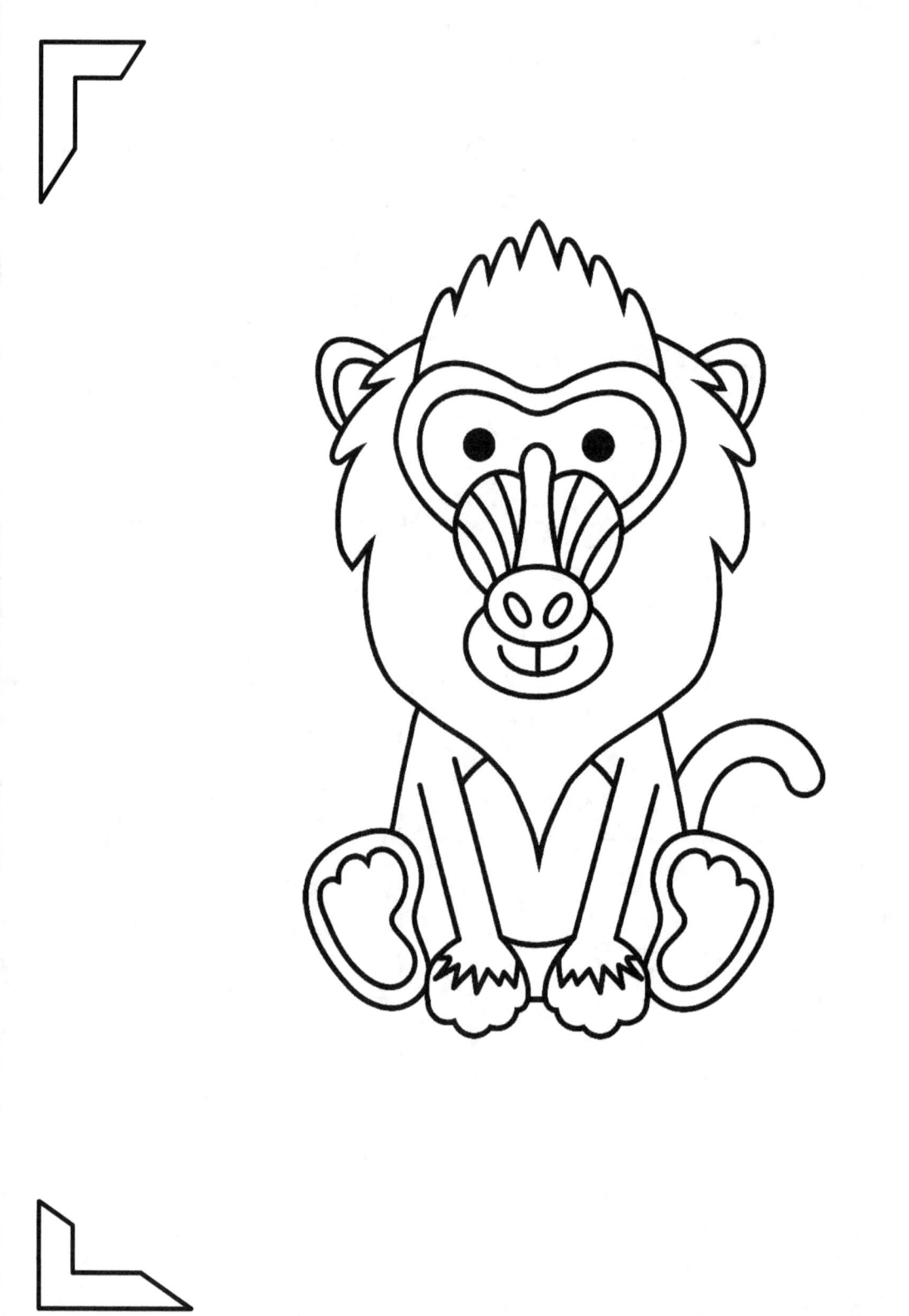

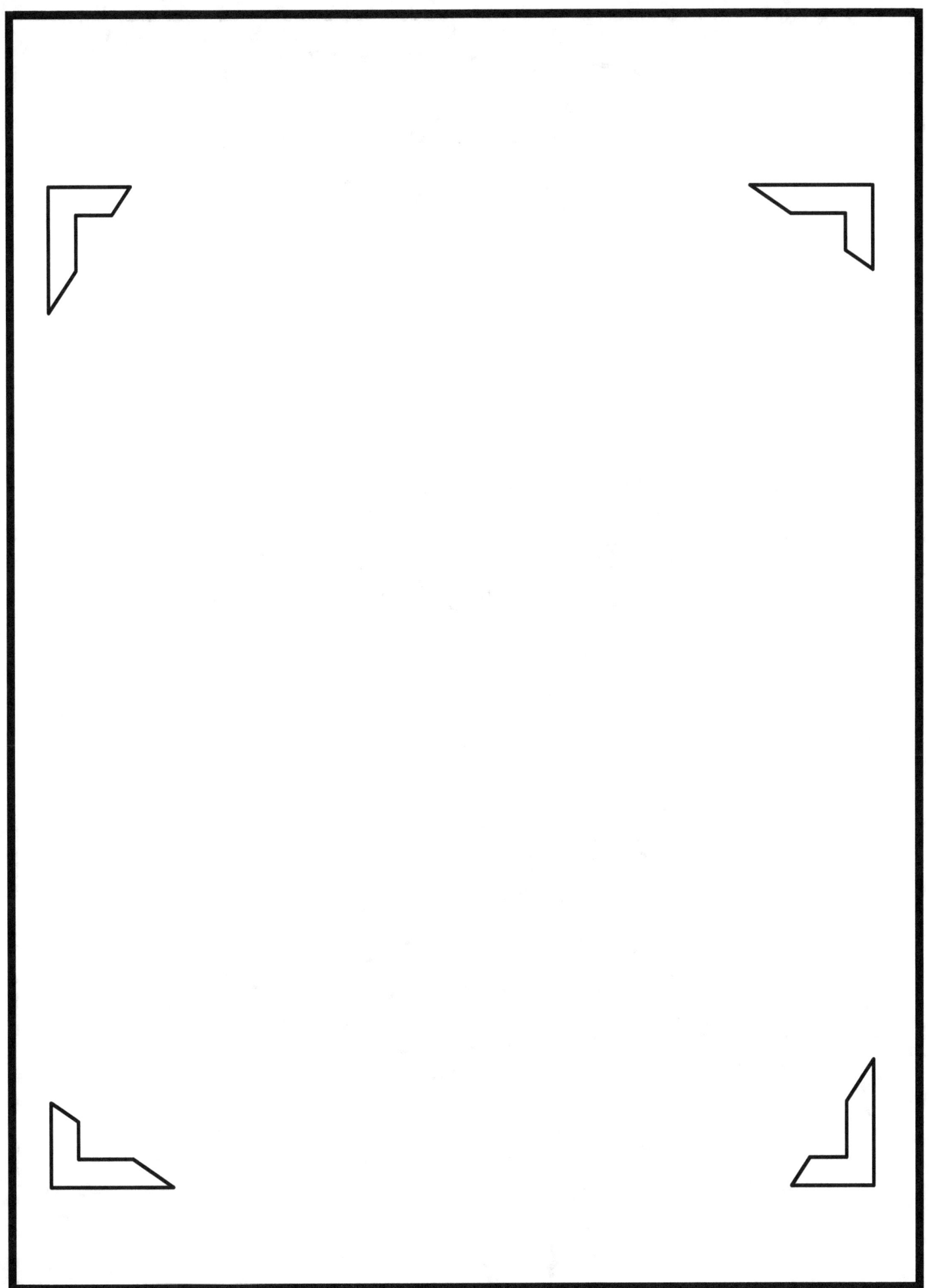

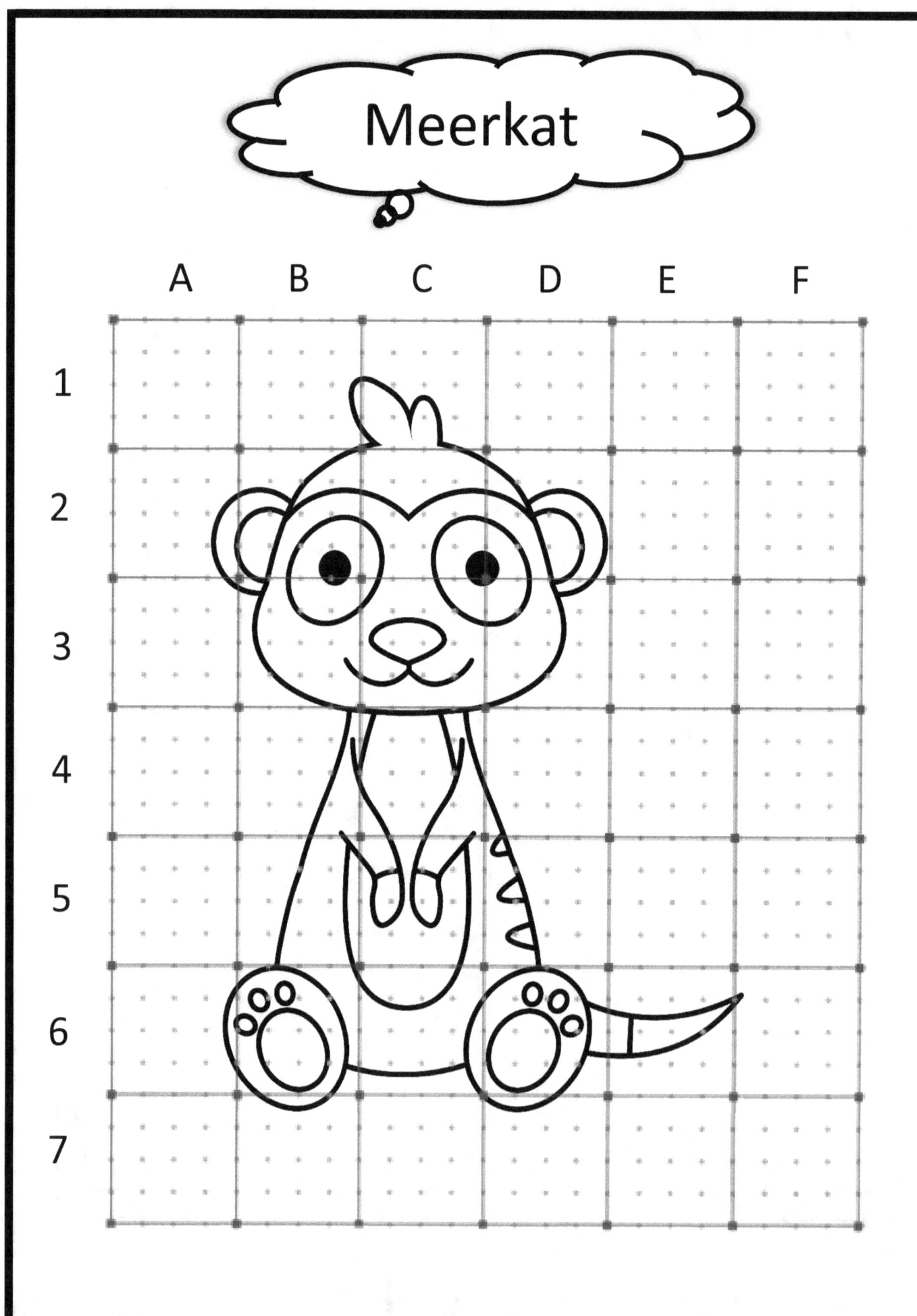

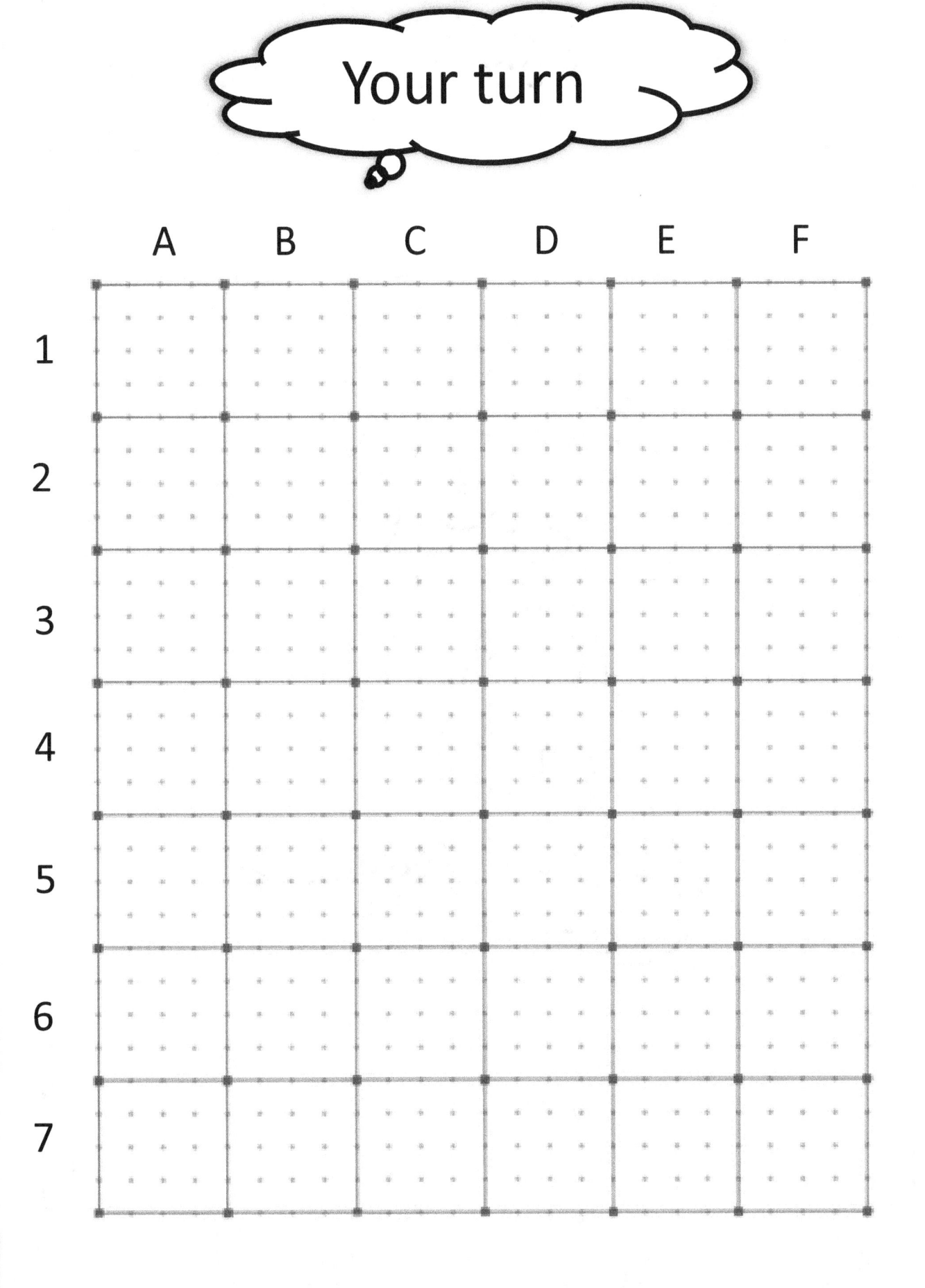

Trace It

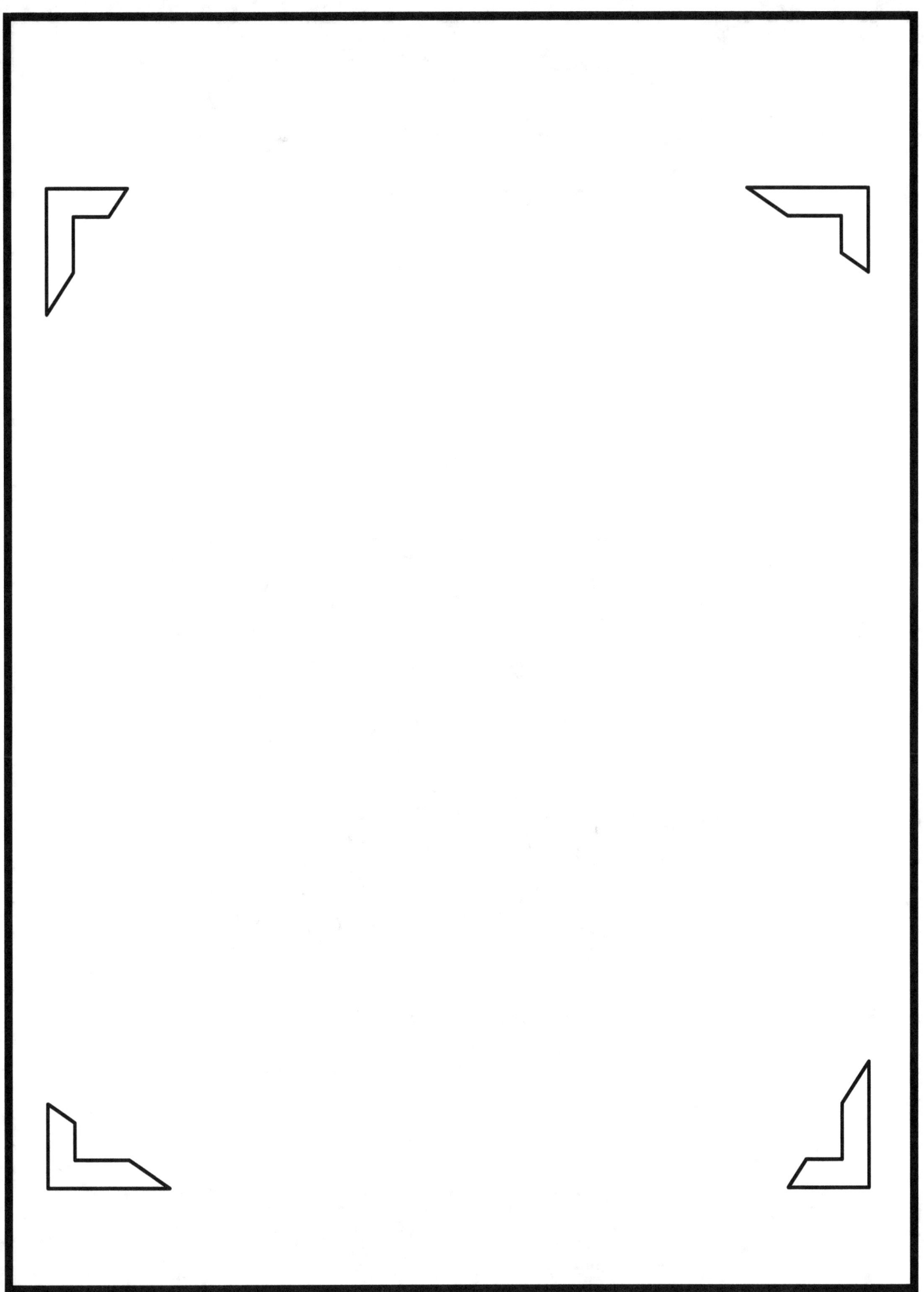

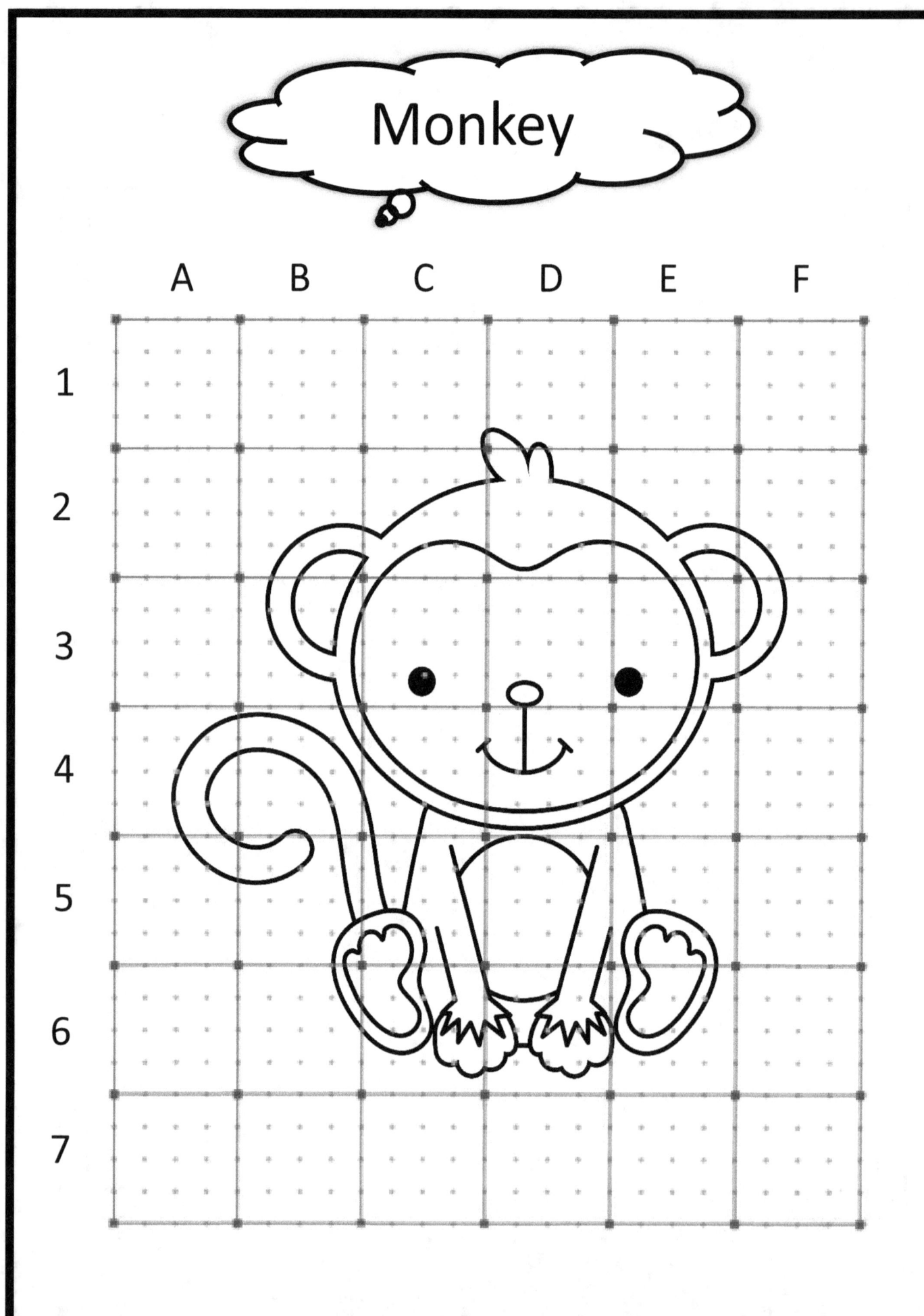

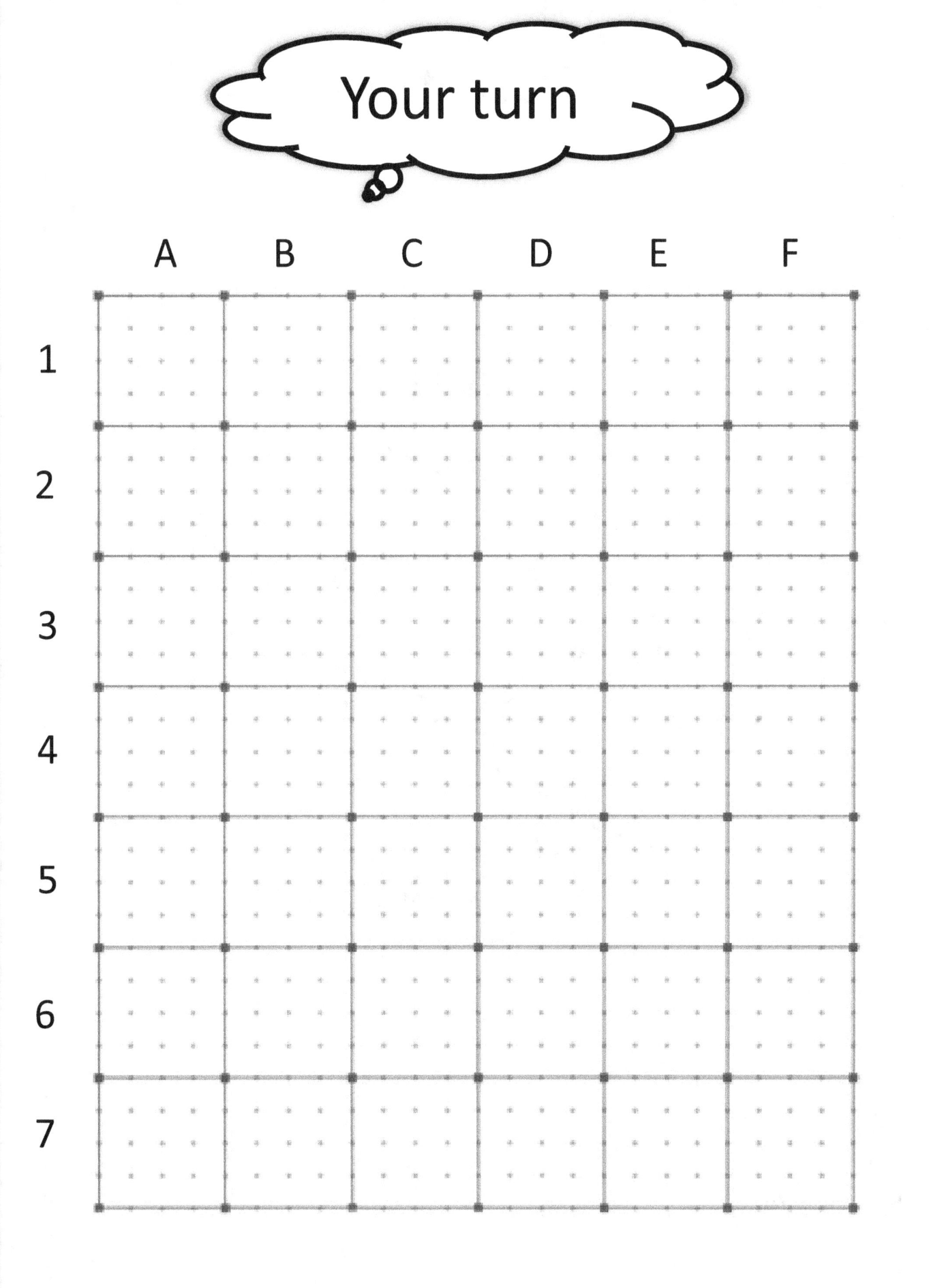

Trace It

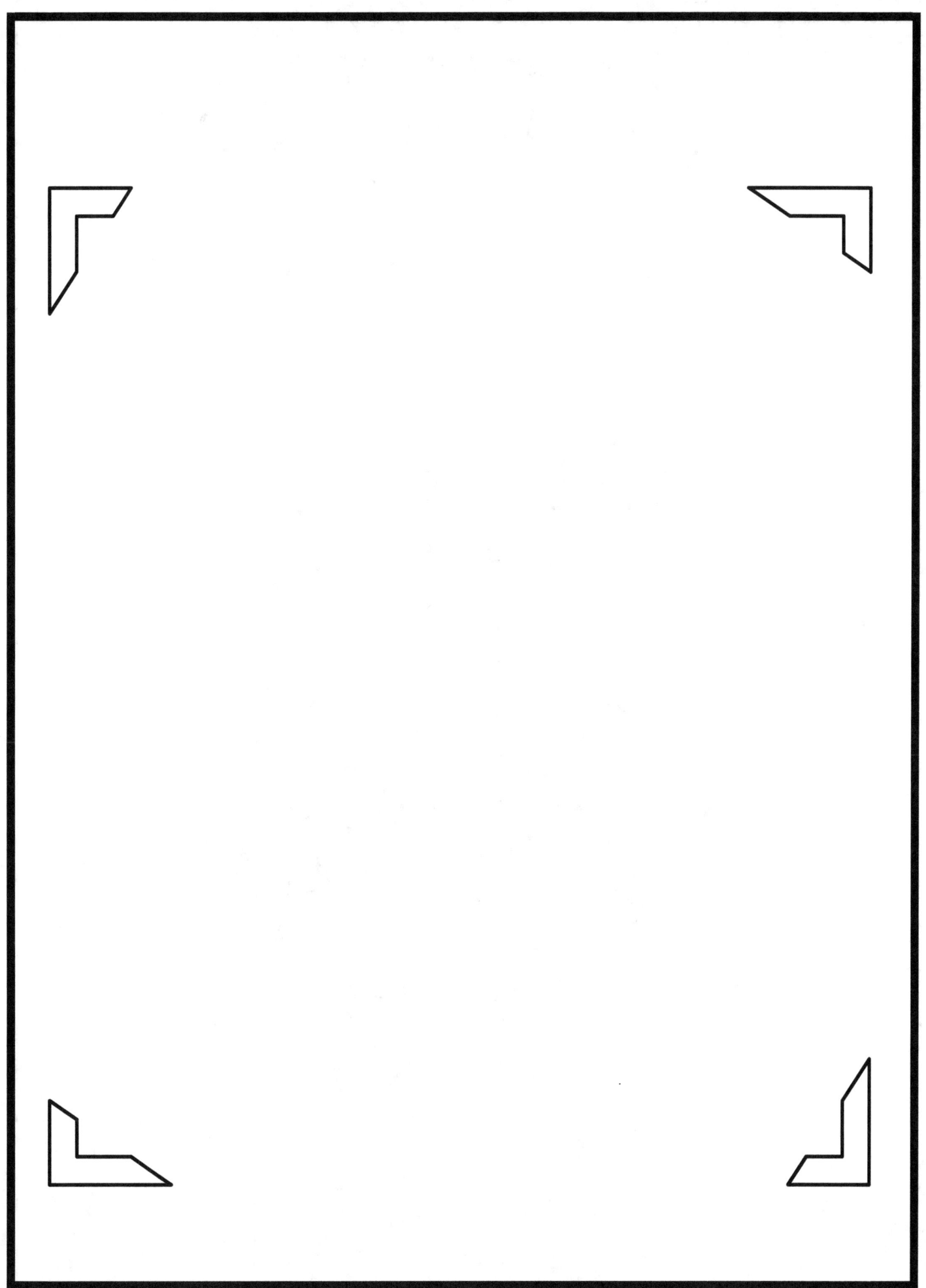

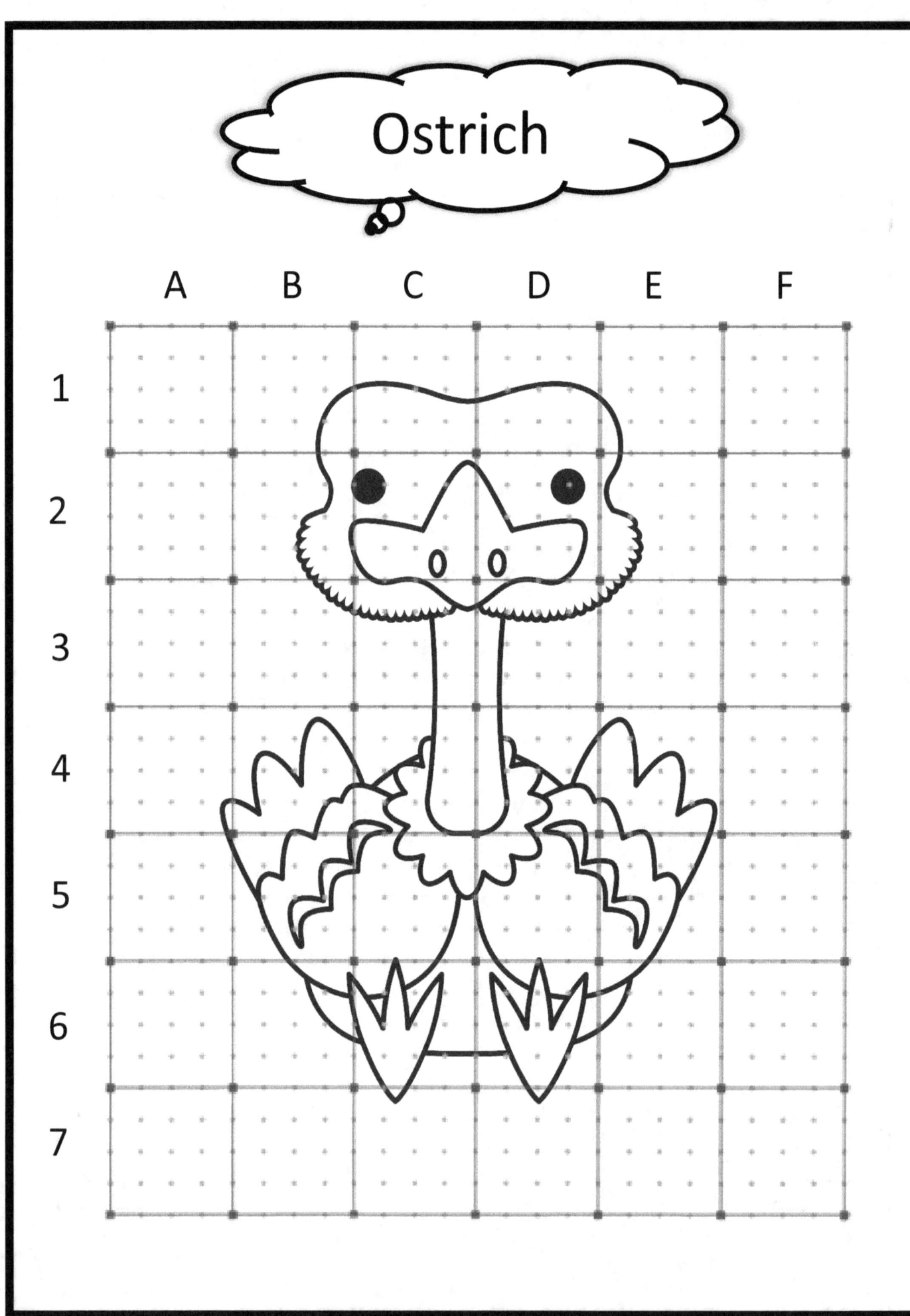

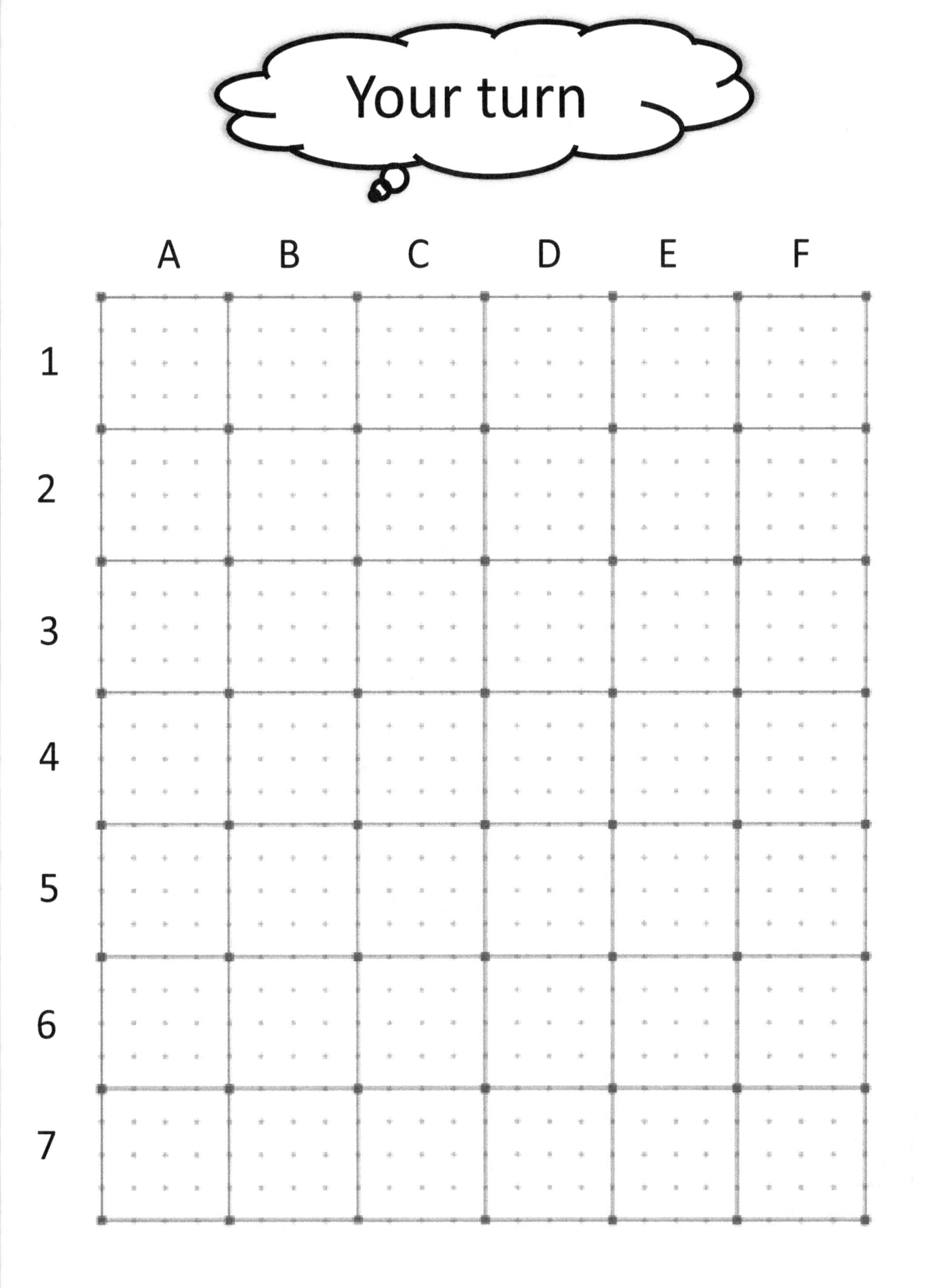

Trace It

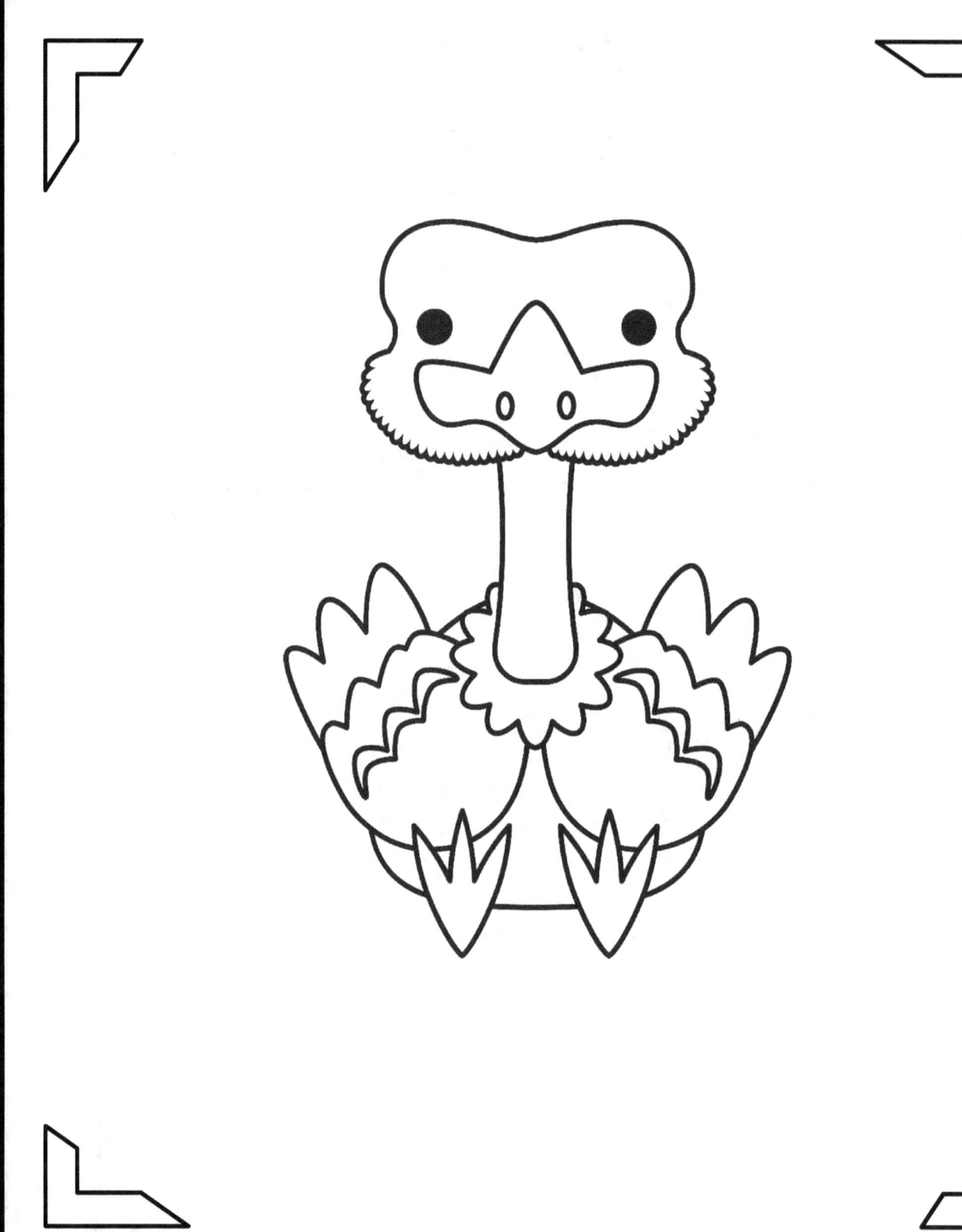

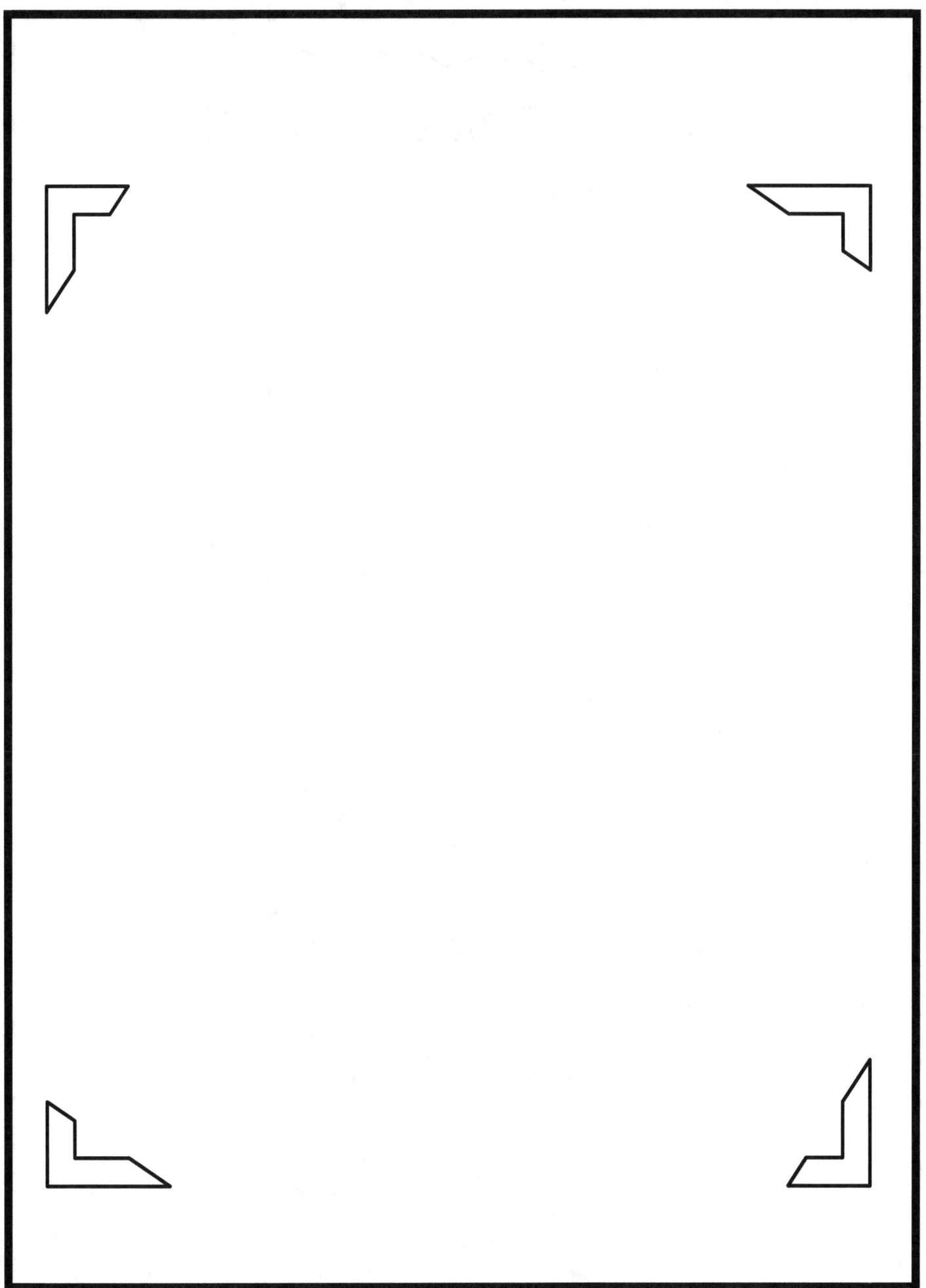

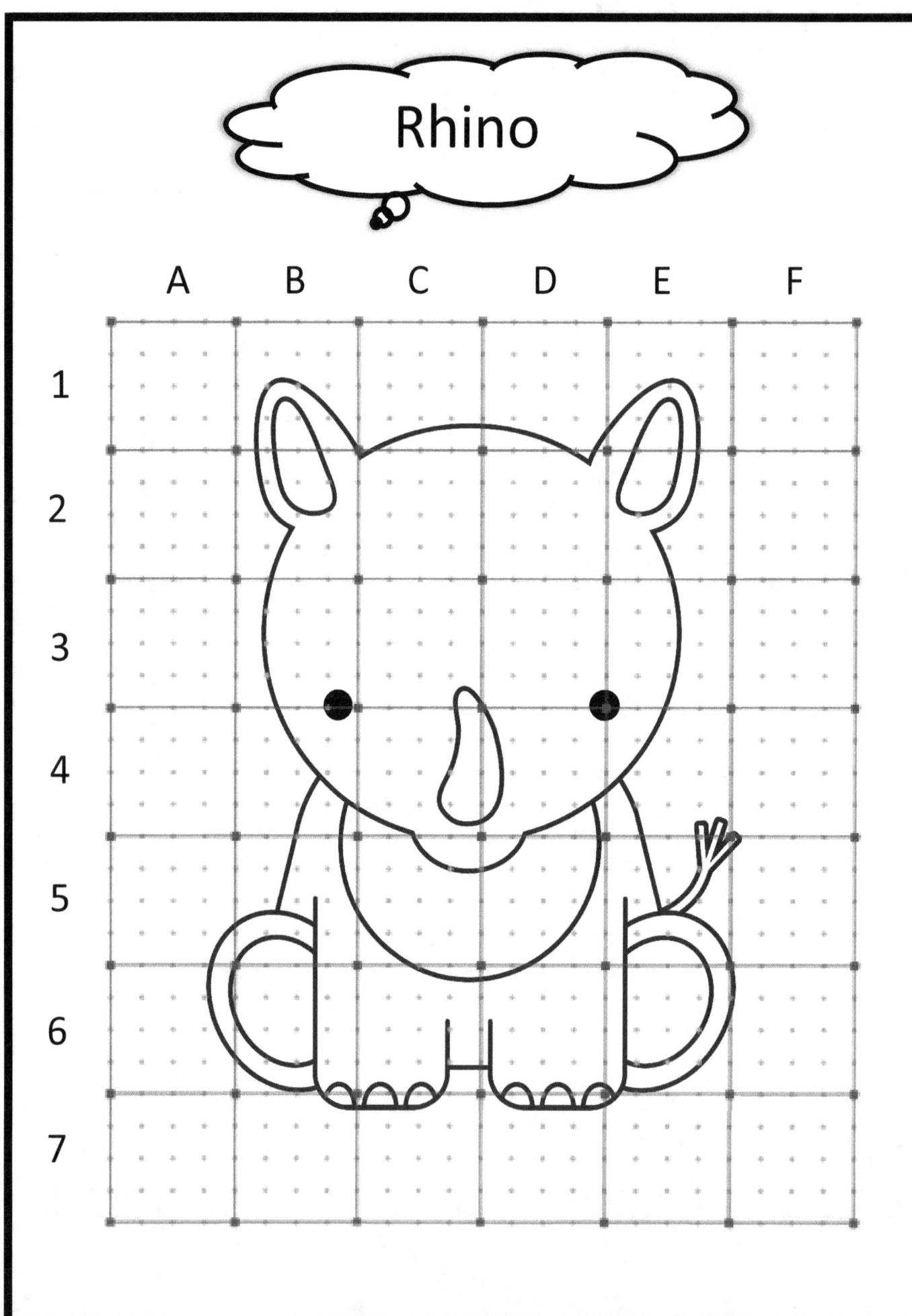

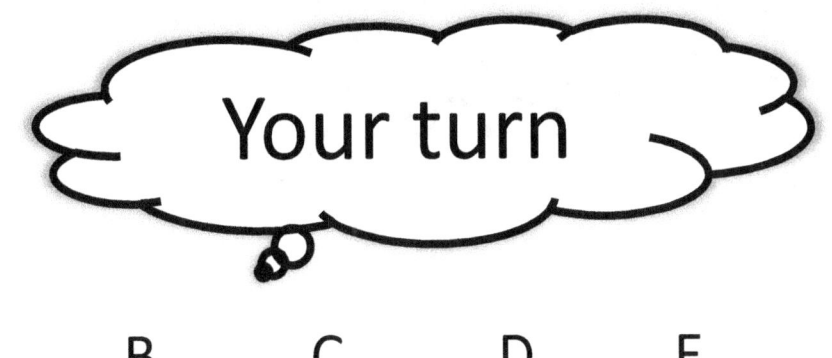

	A	B	C	D	E	F
1						
2						
3						
4						
5						
6						
7						

Trace It

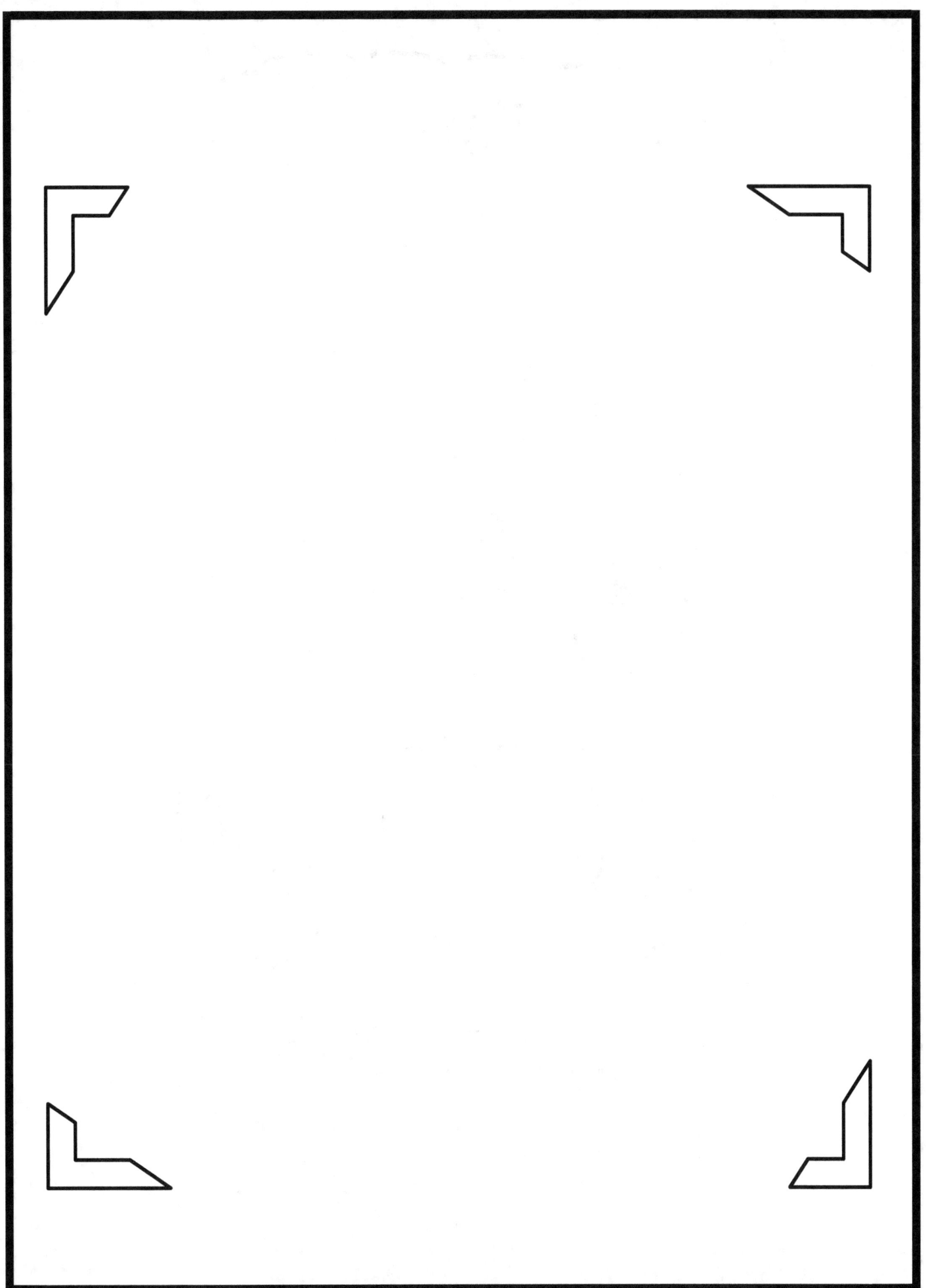

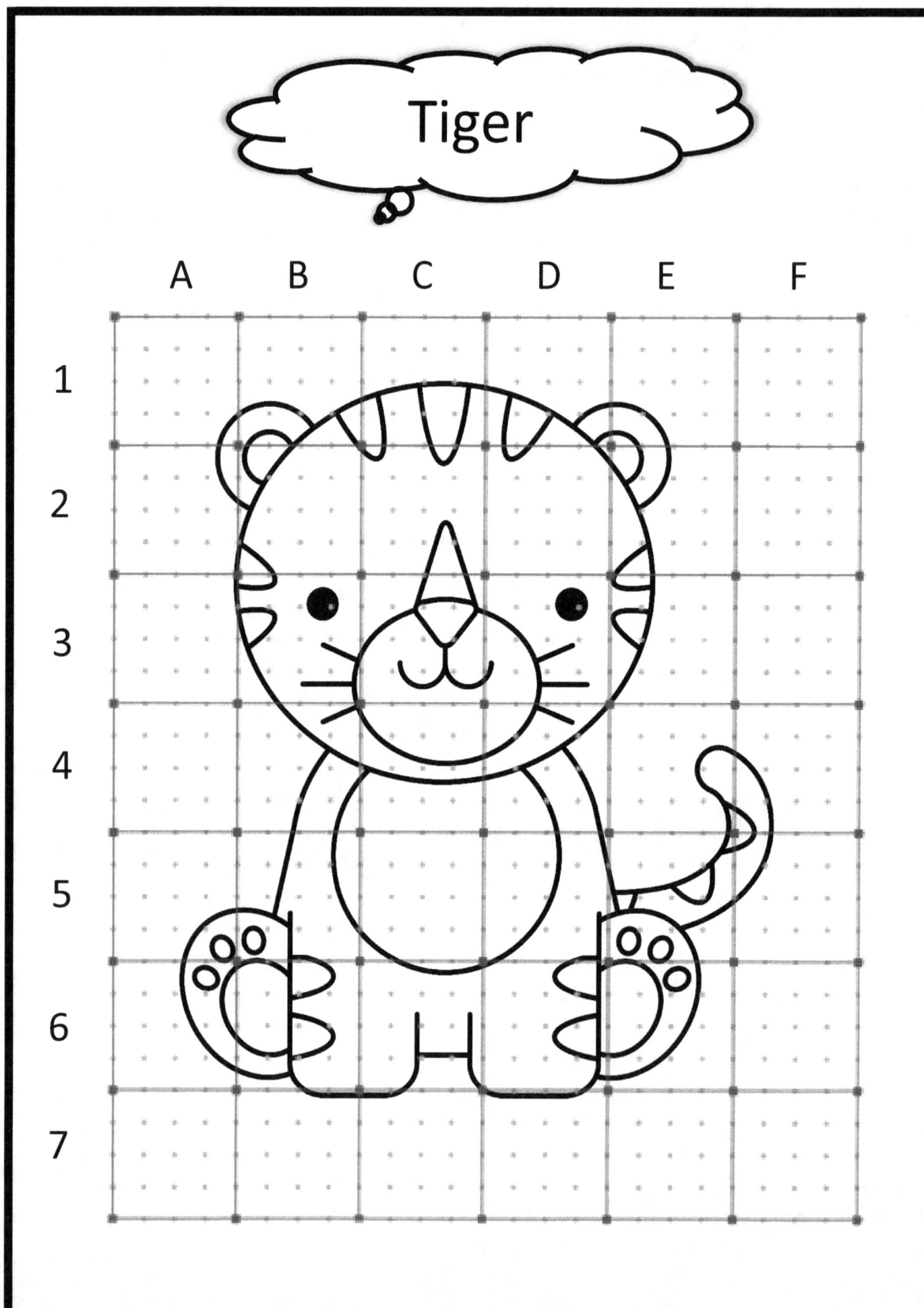

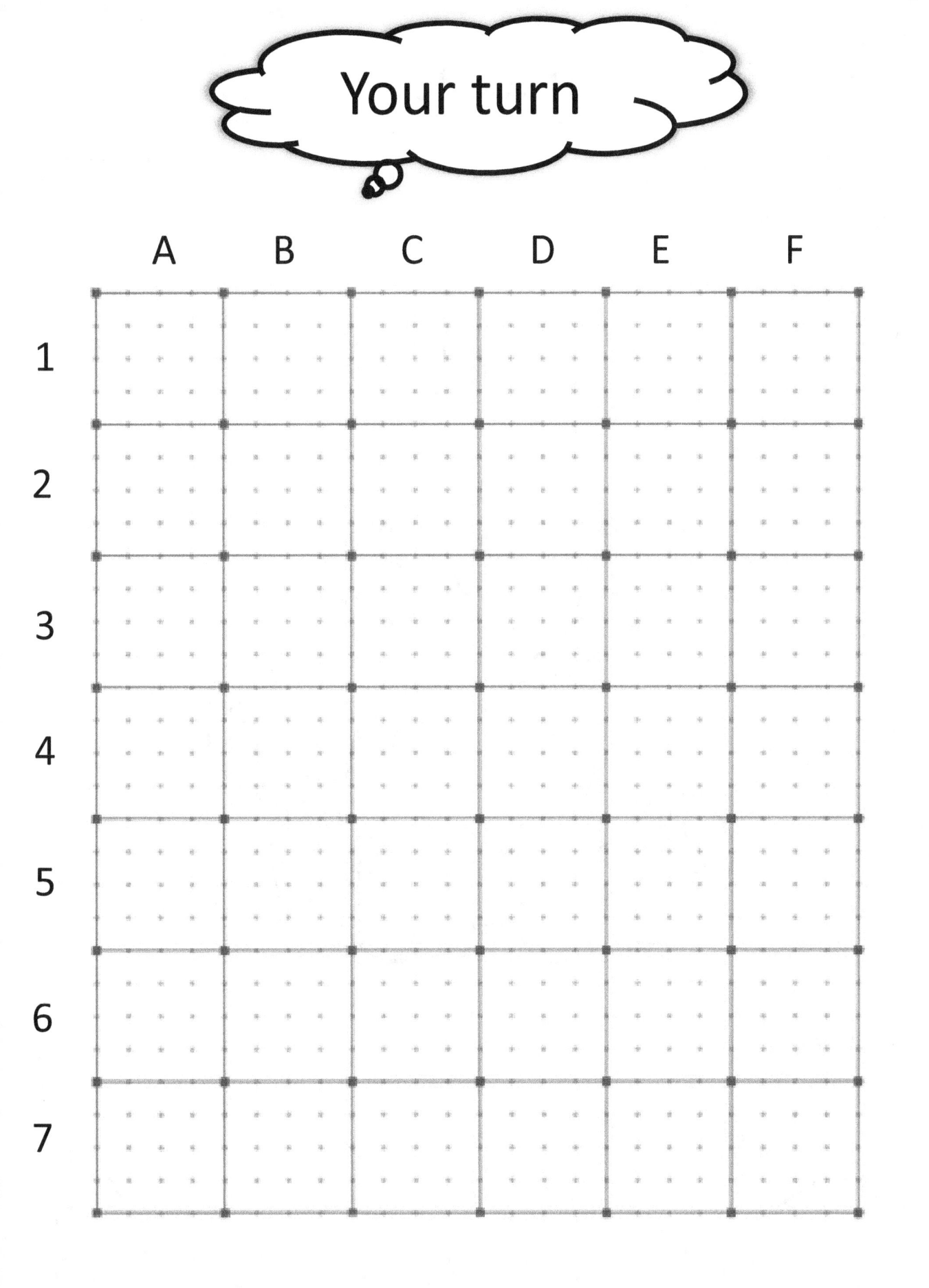

Trace It

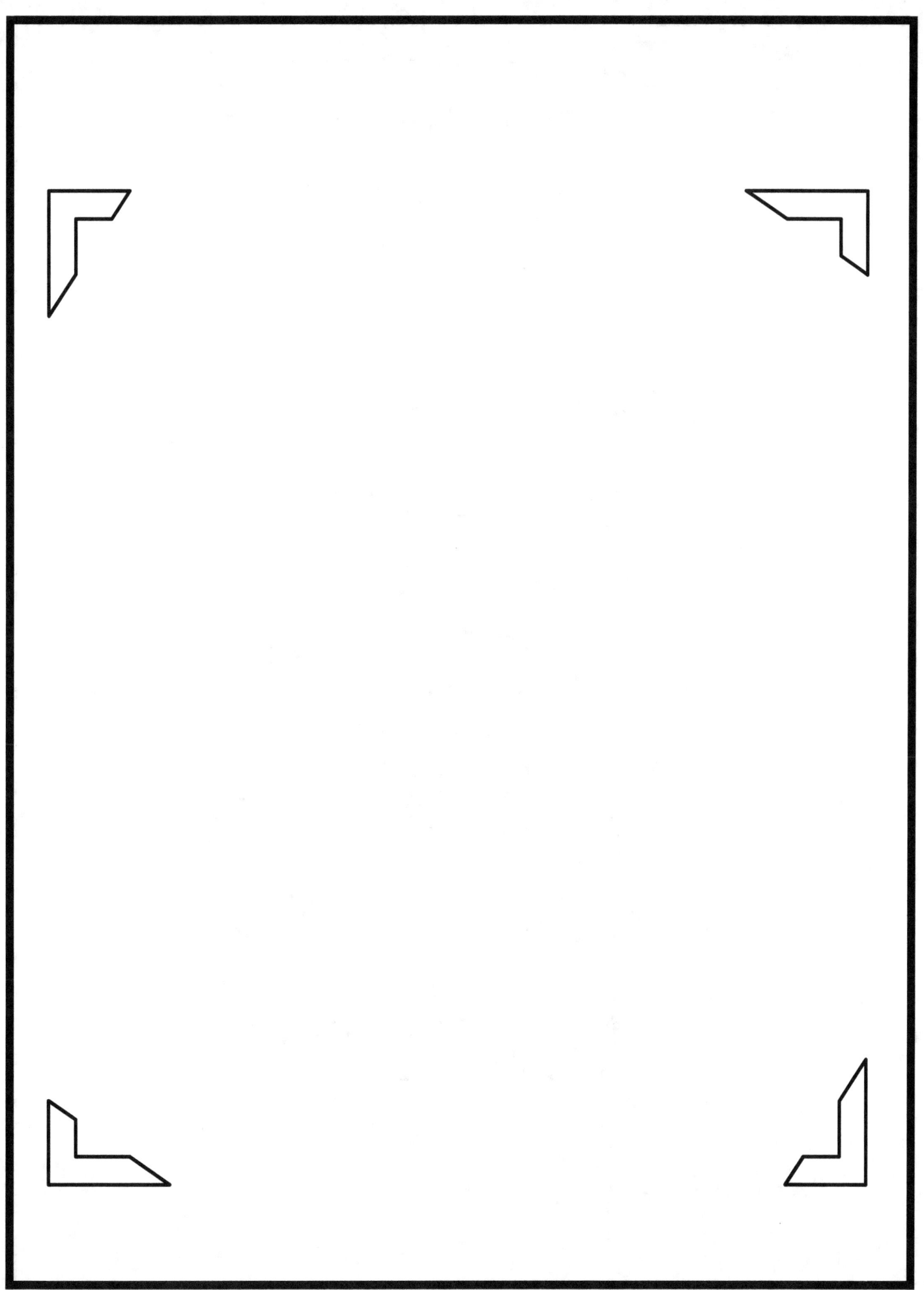

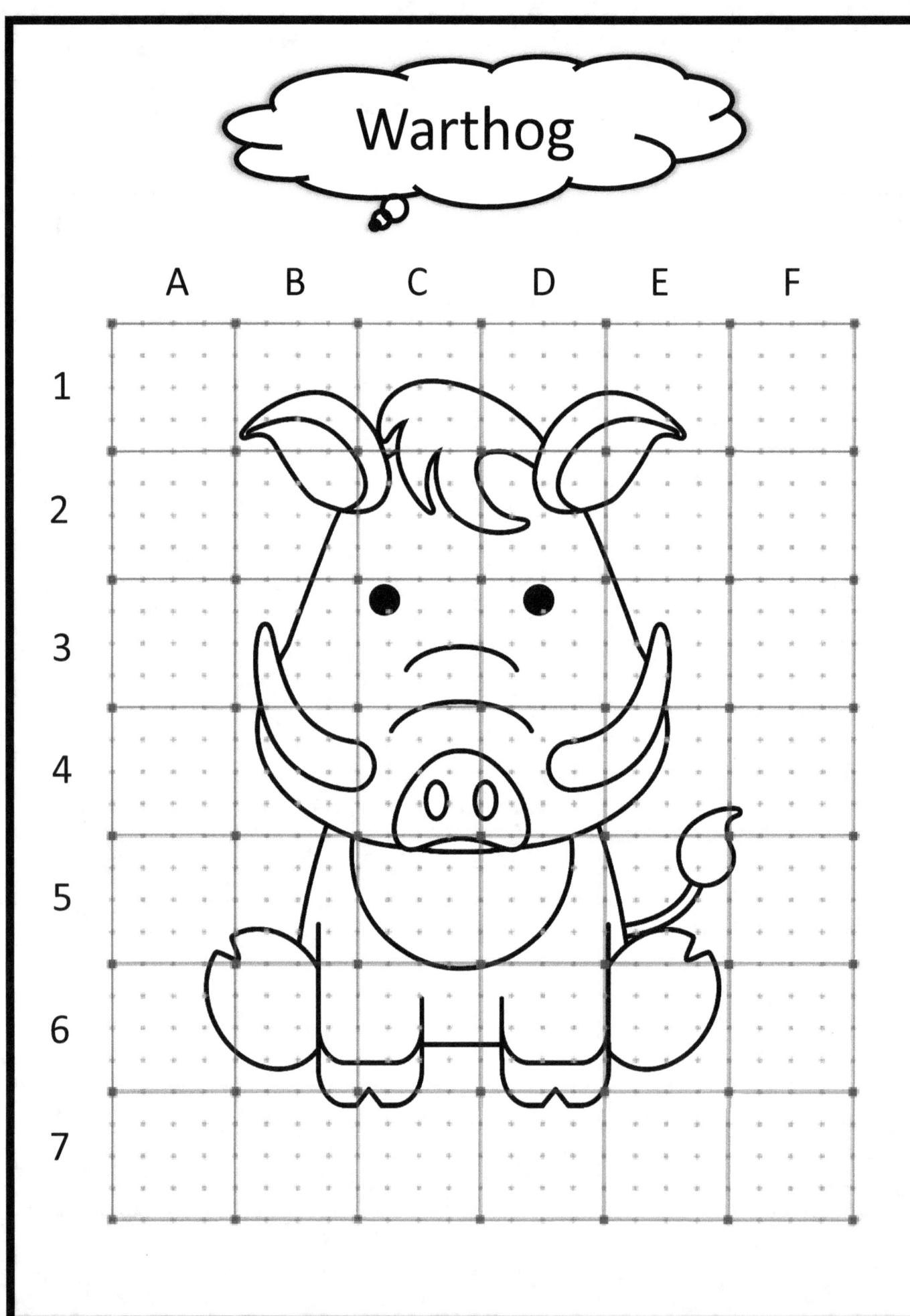

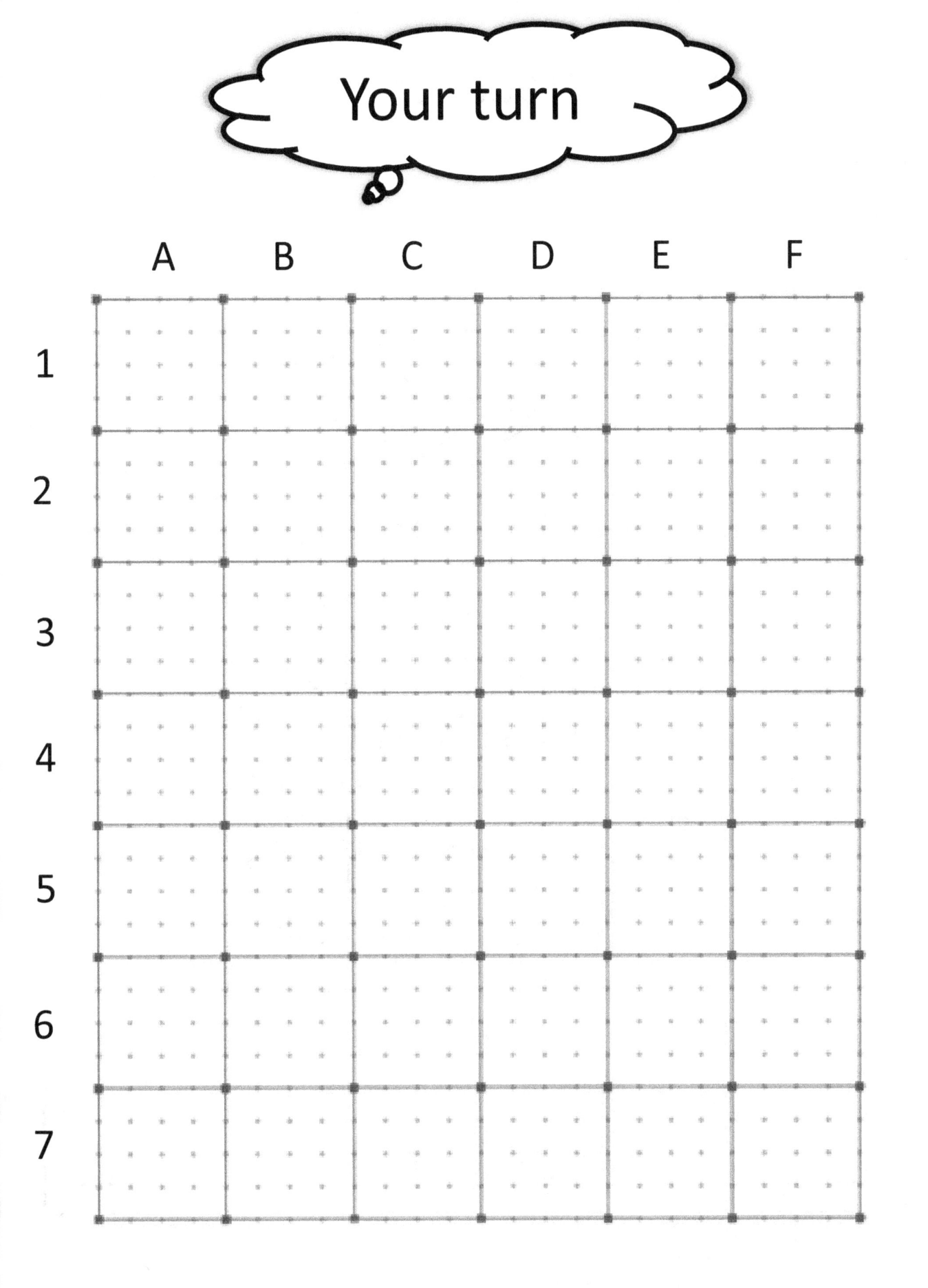

Trace It

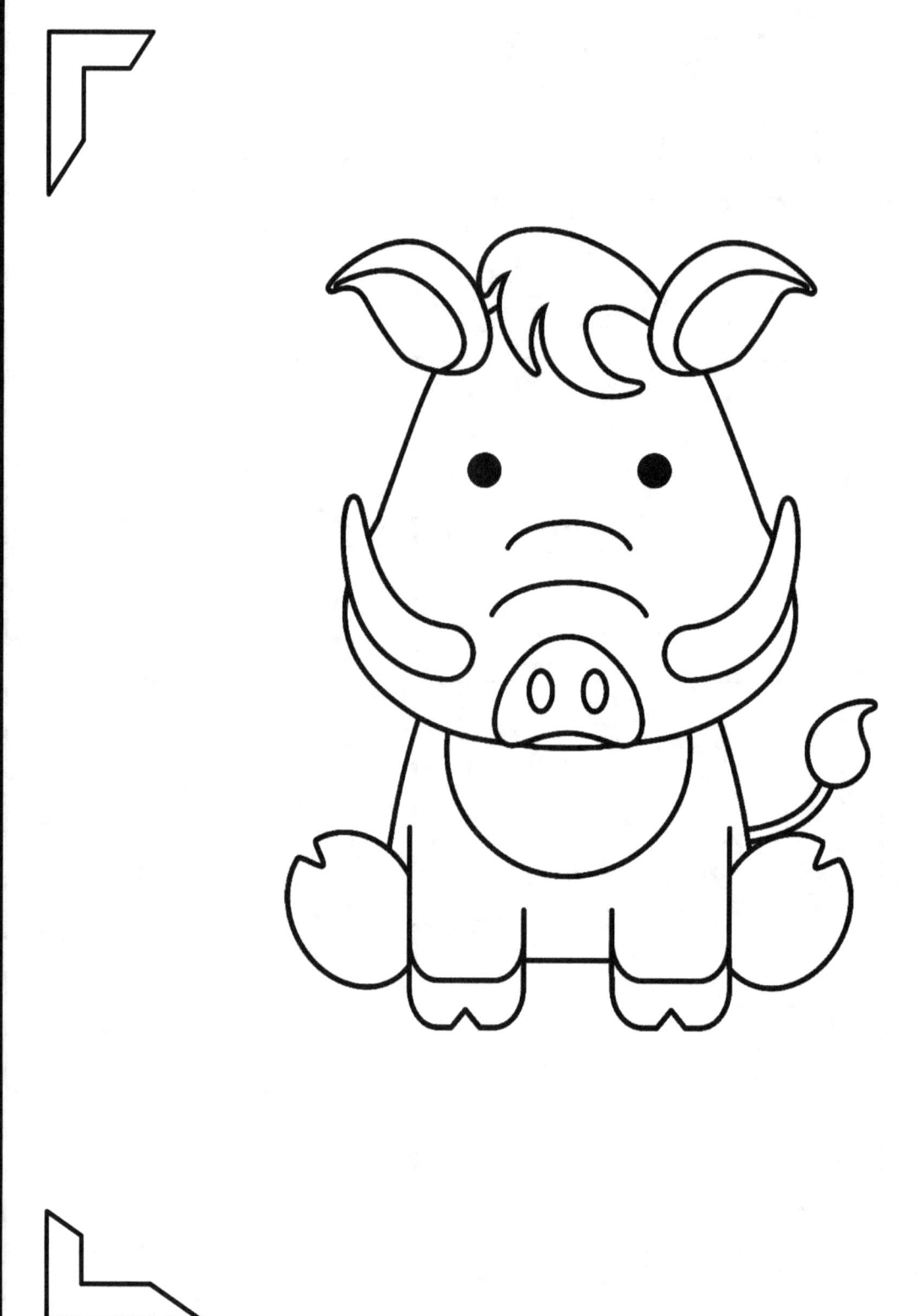

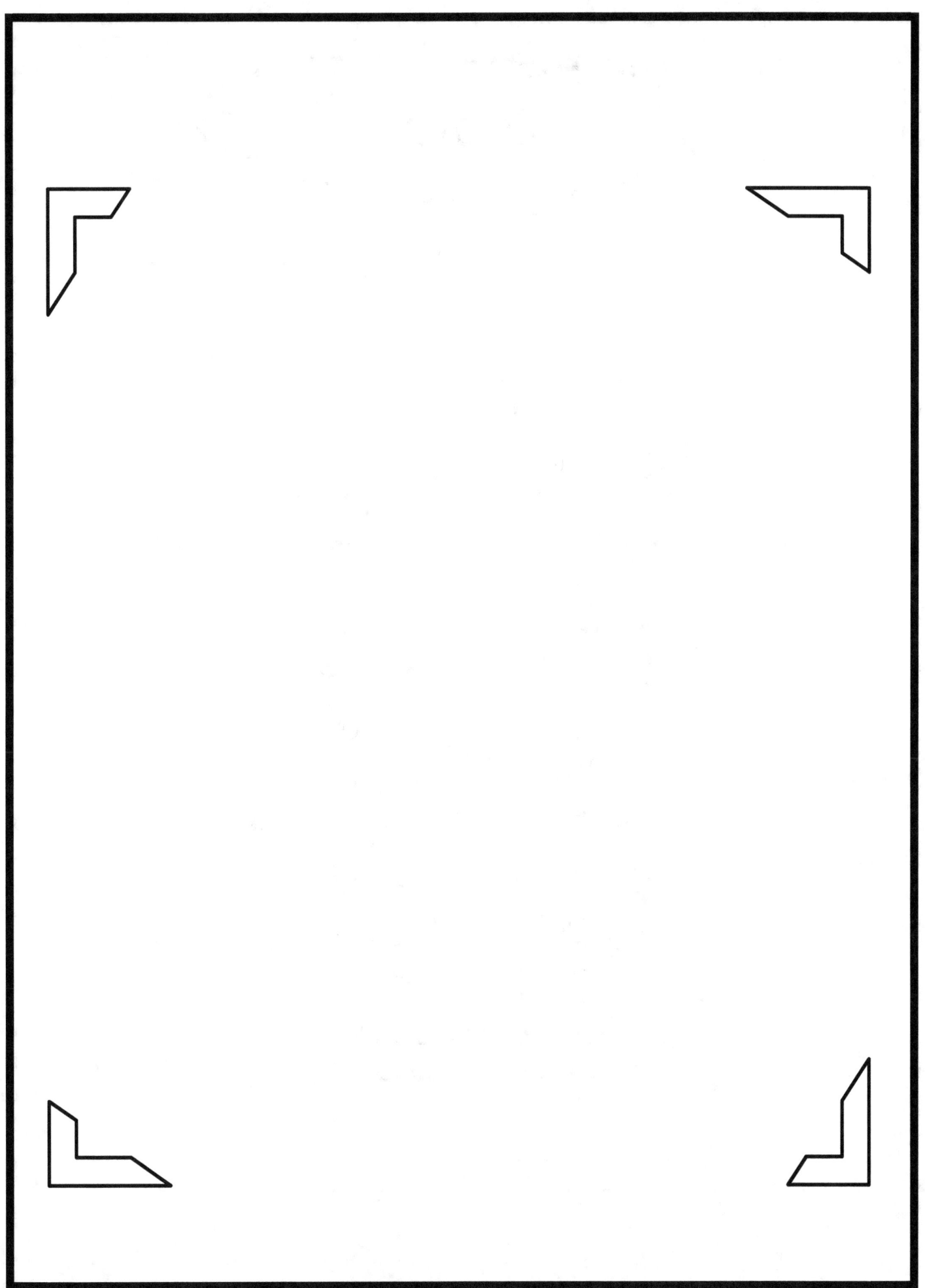

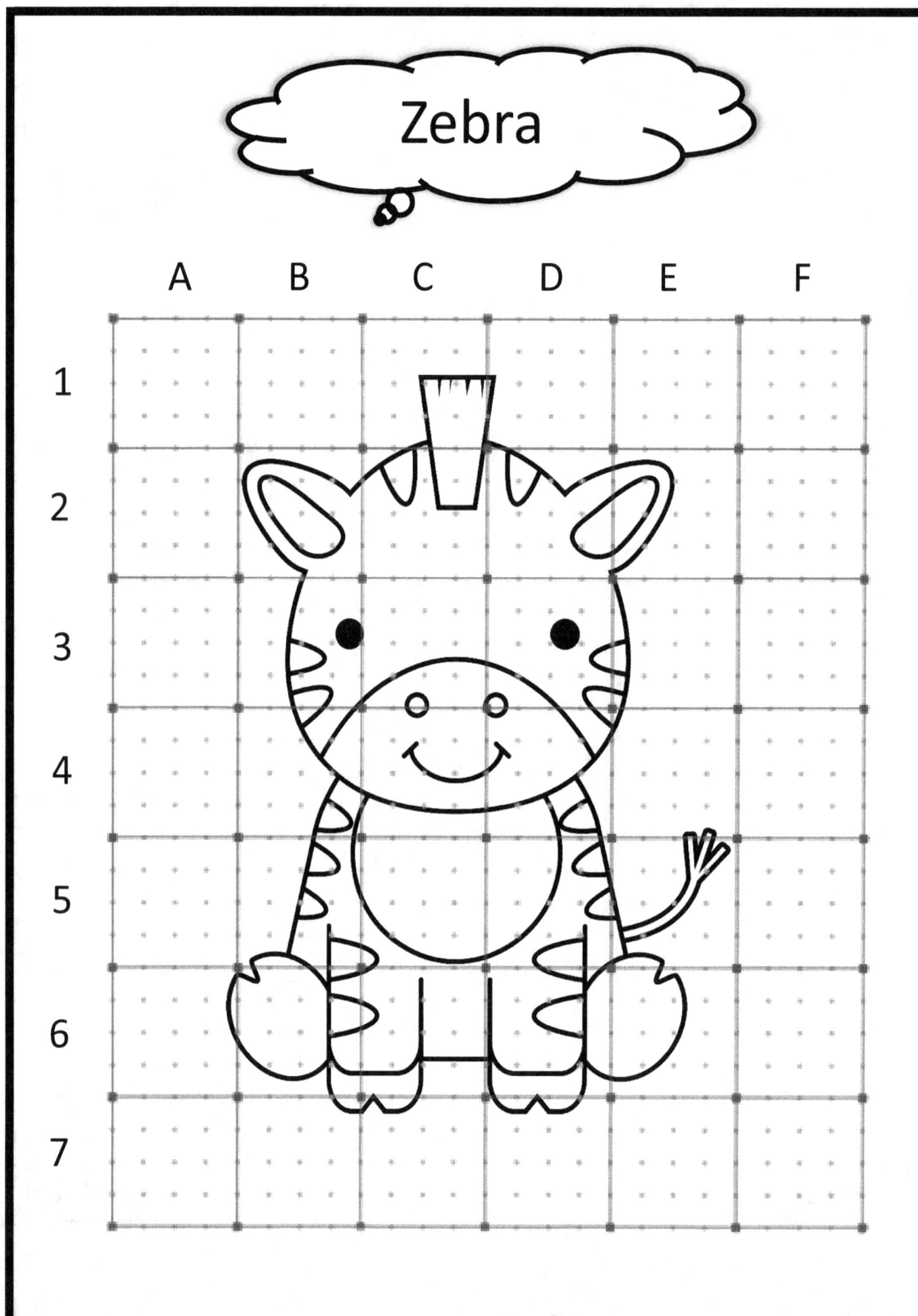

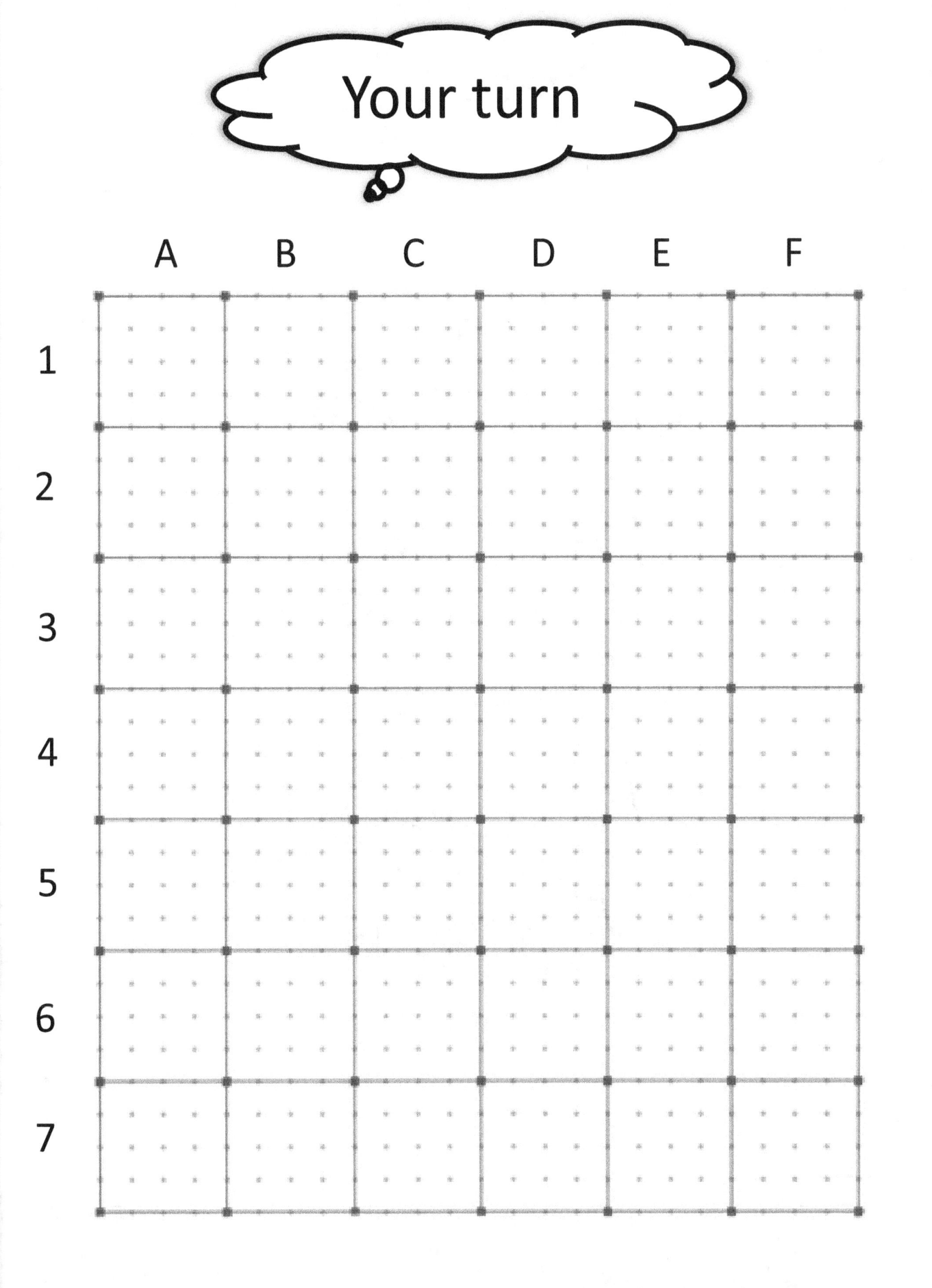

Trace It

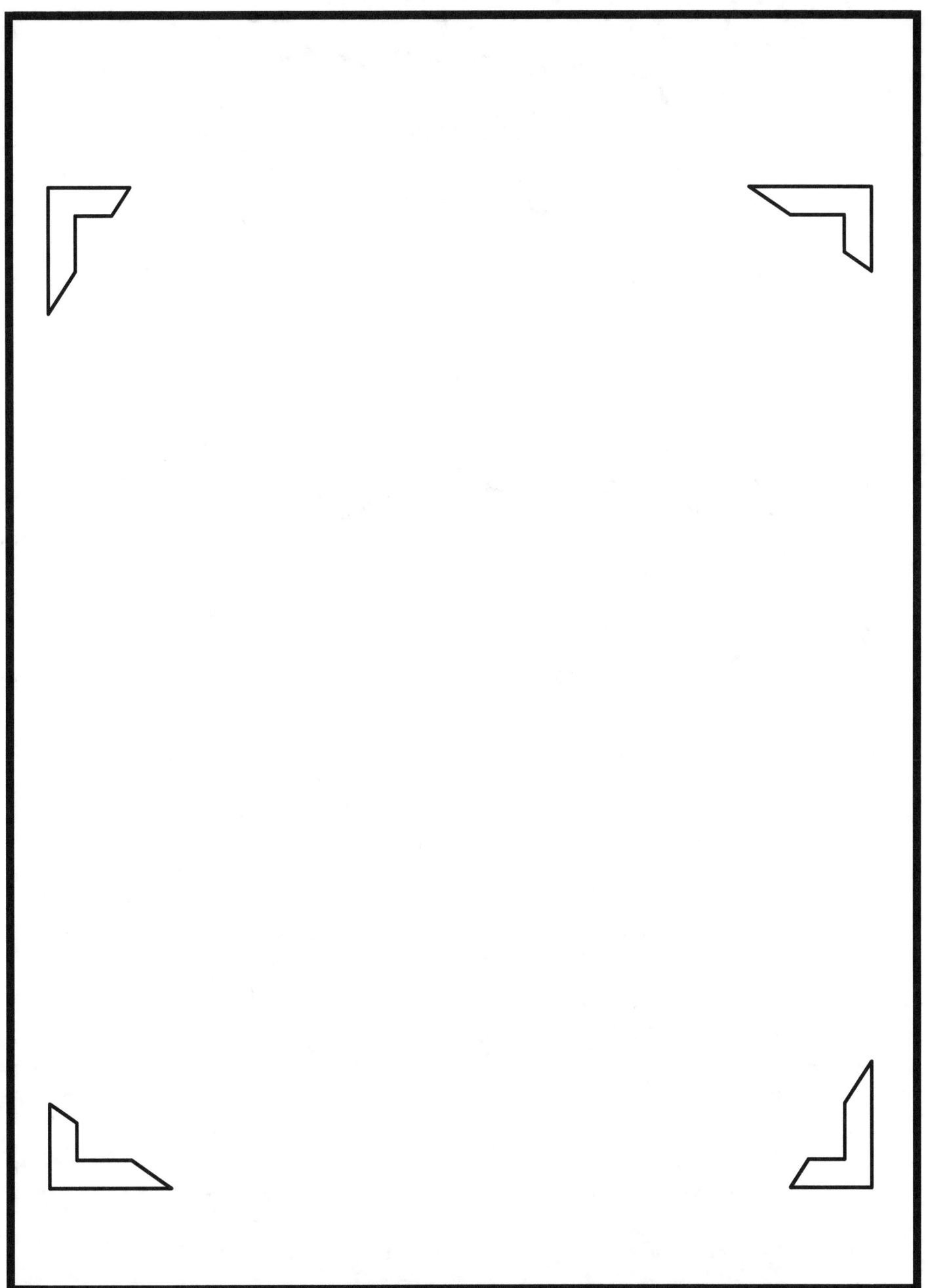

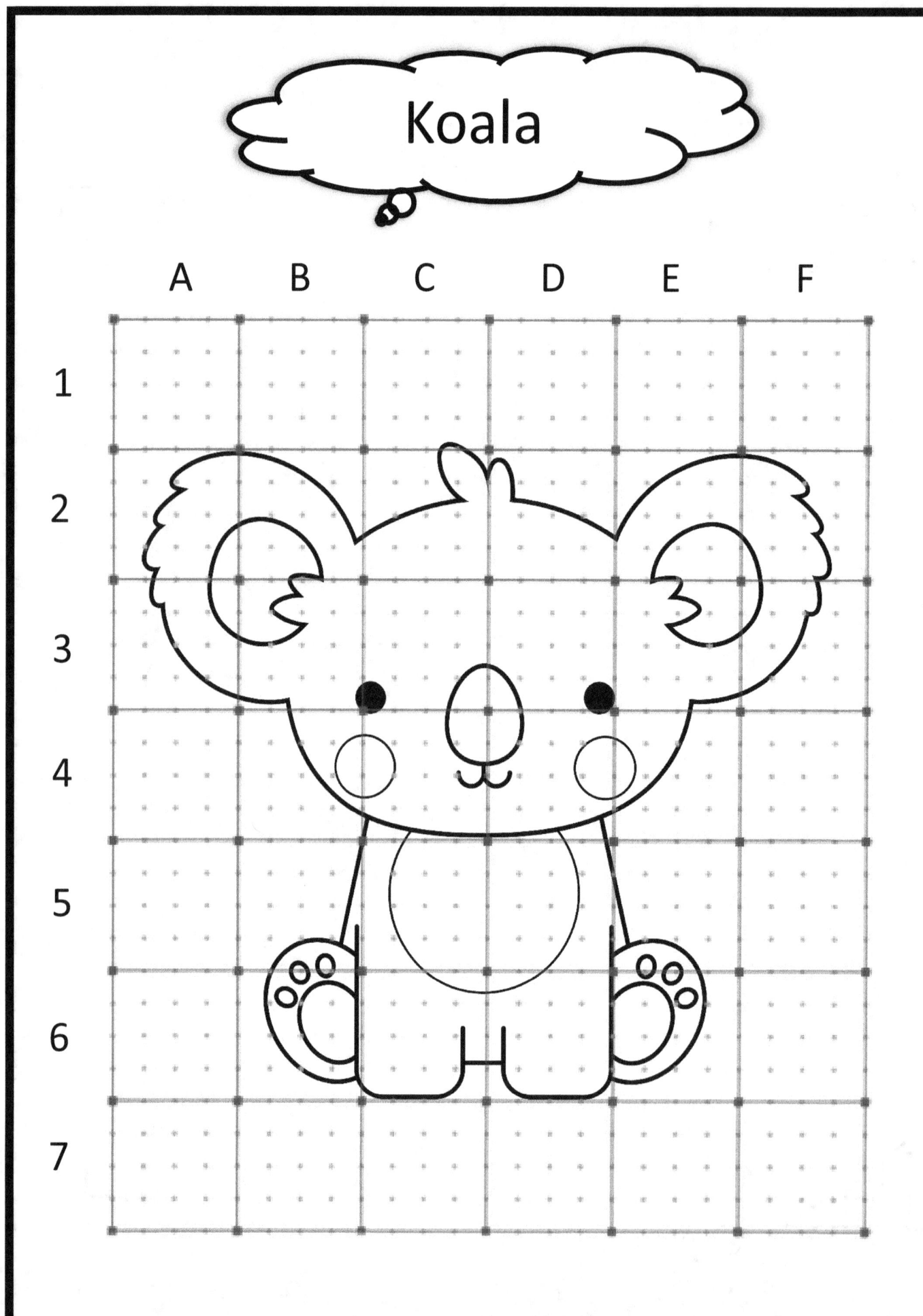

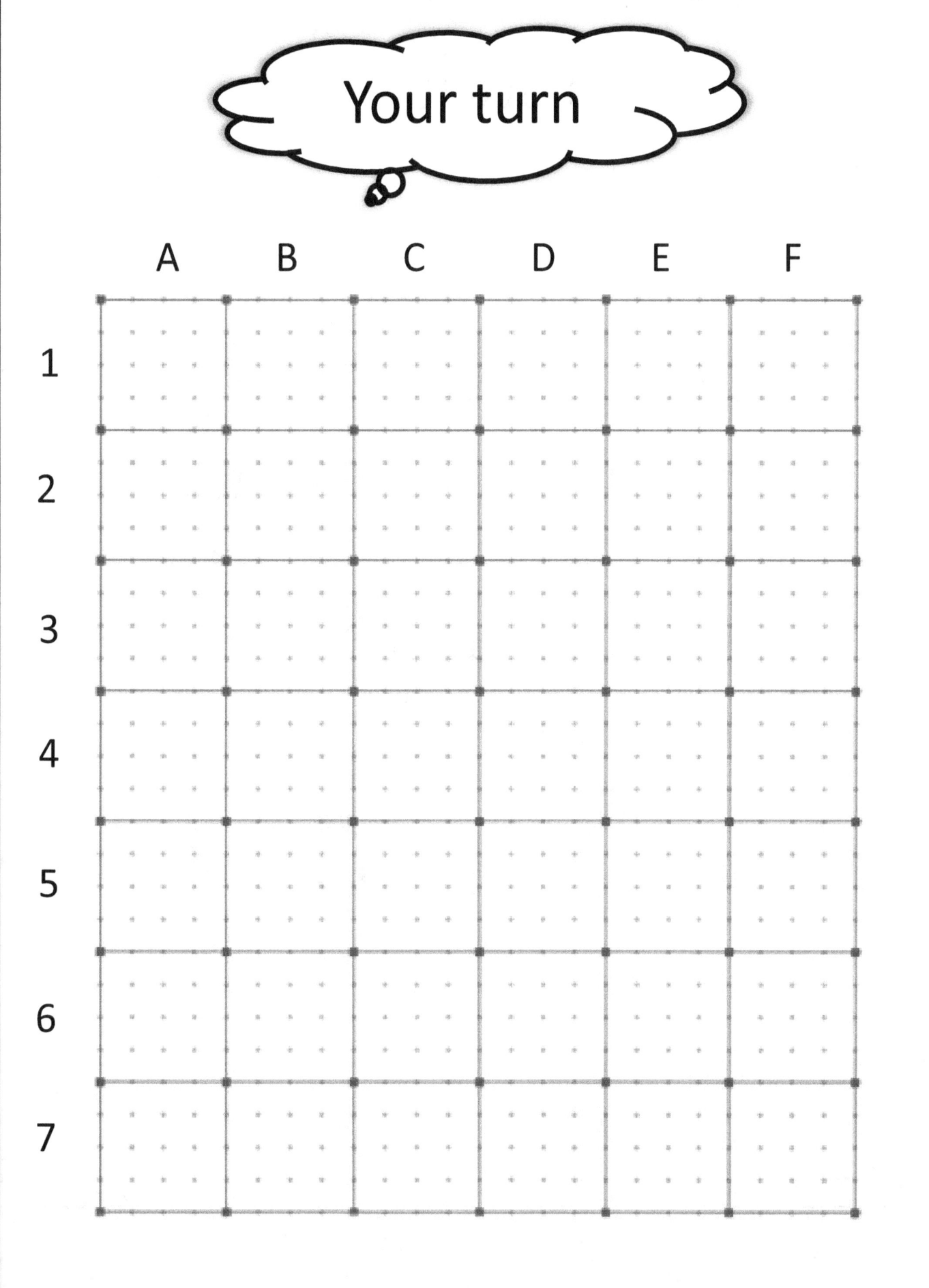

Trace It

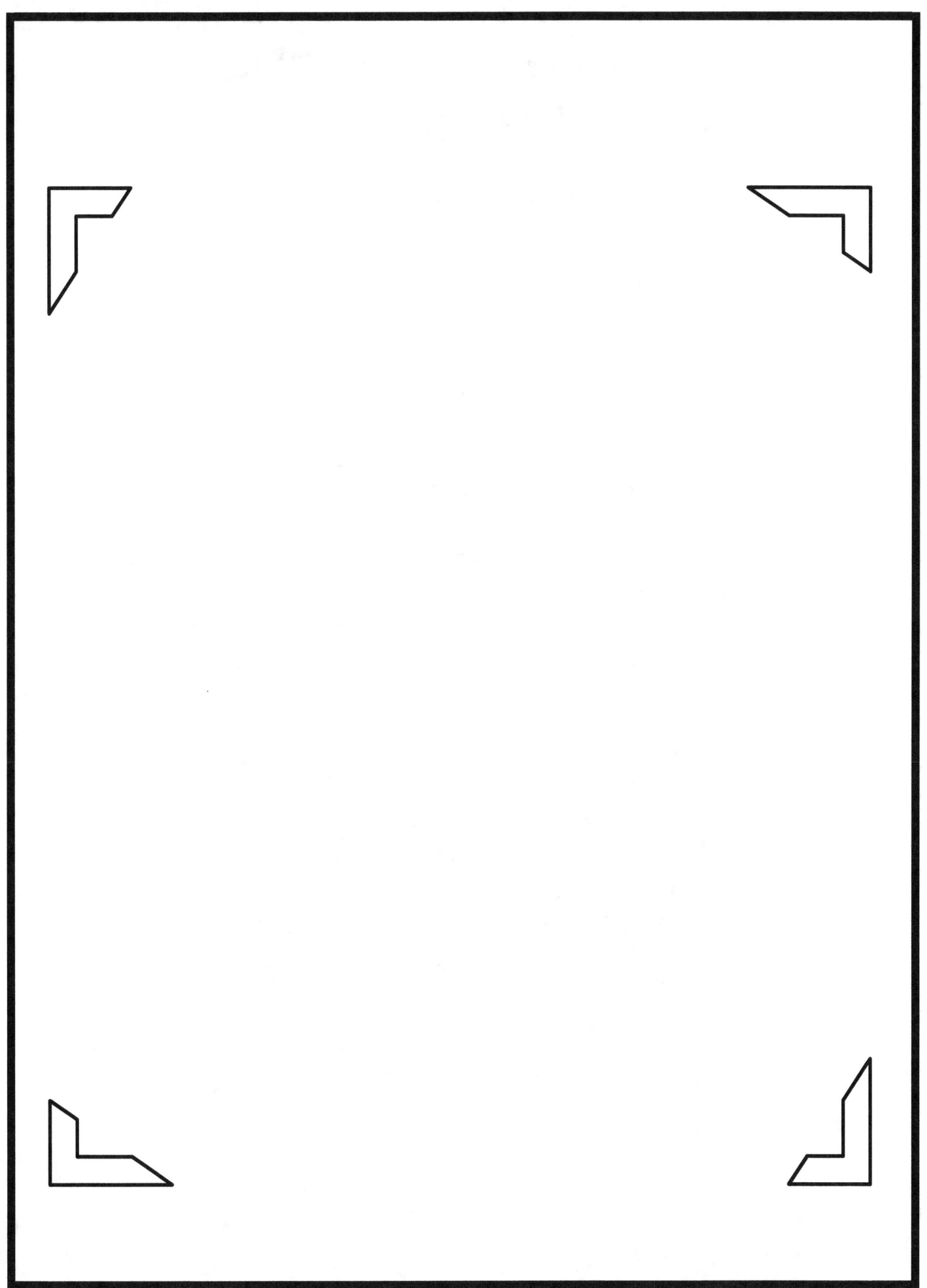

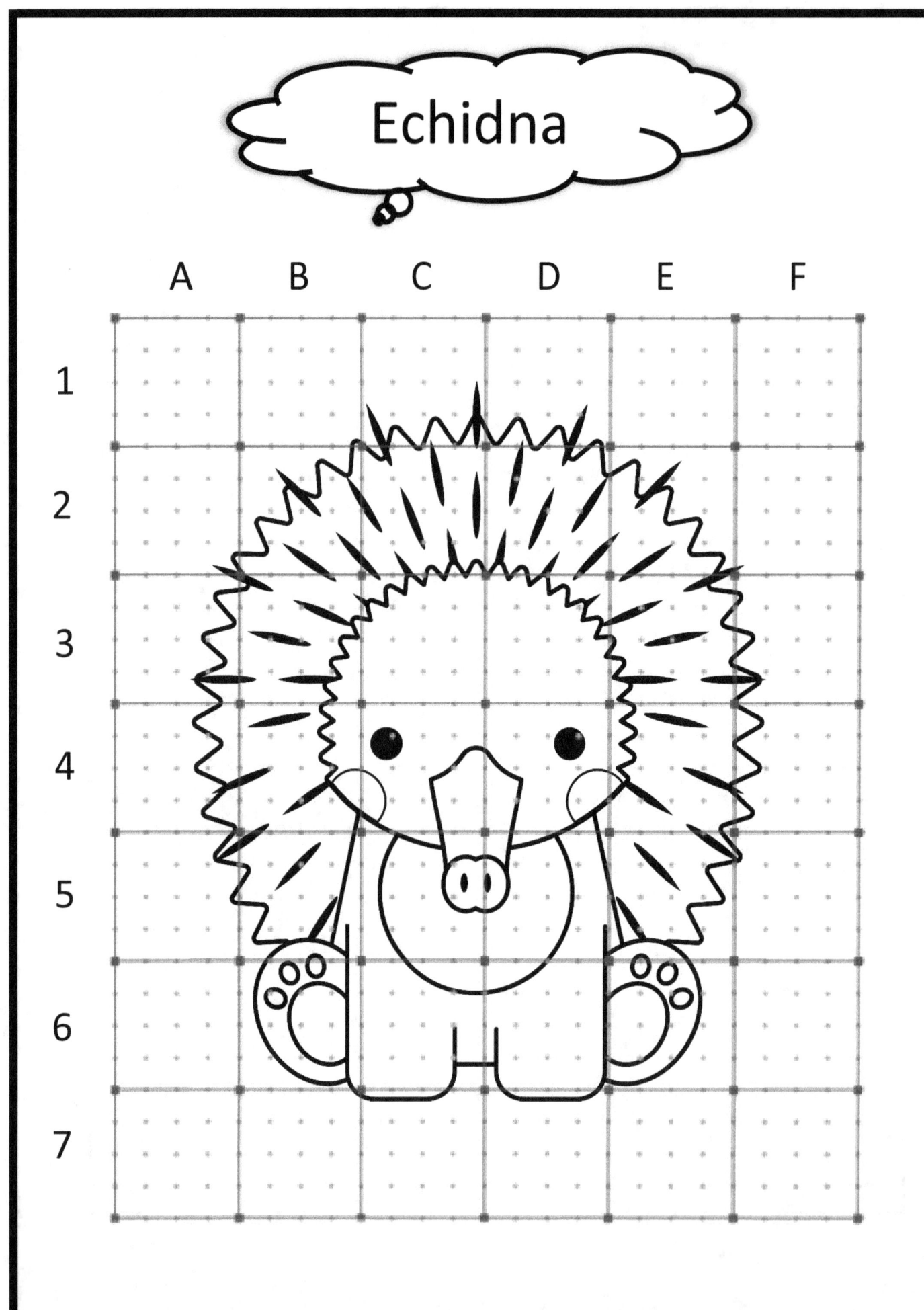

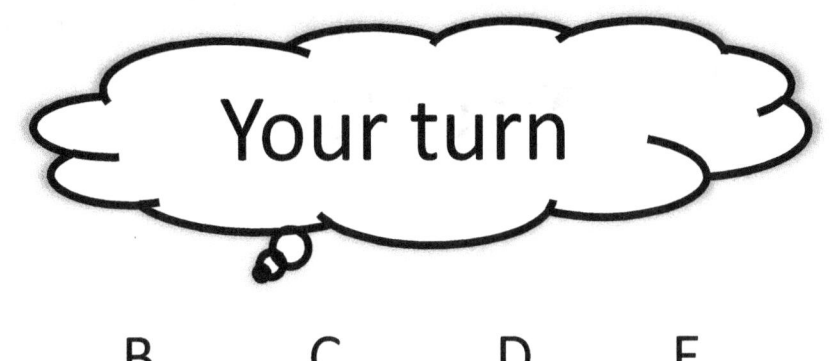

Trace It

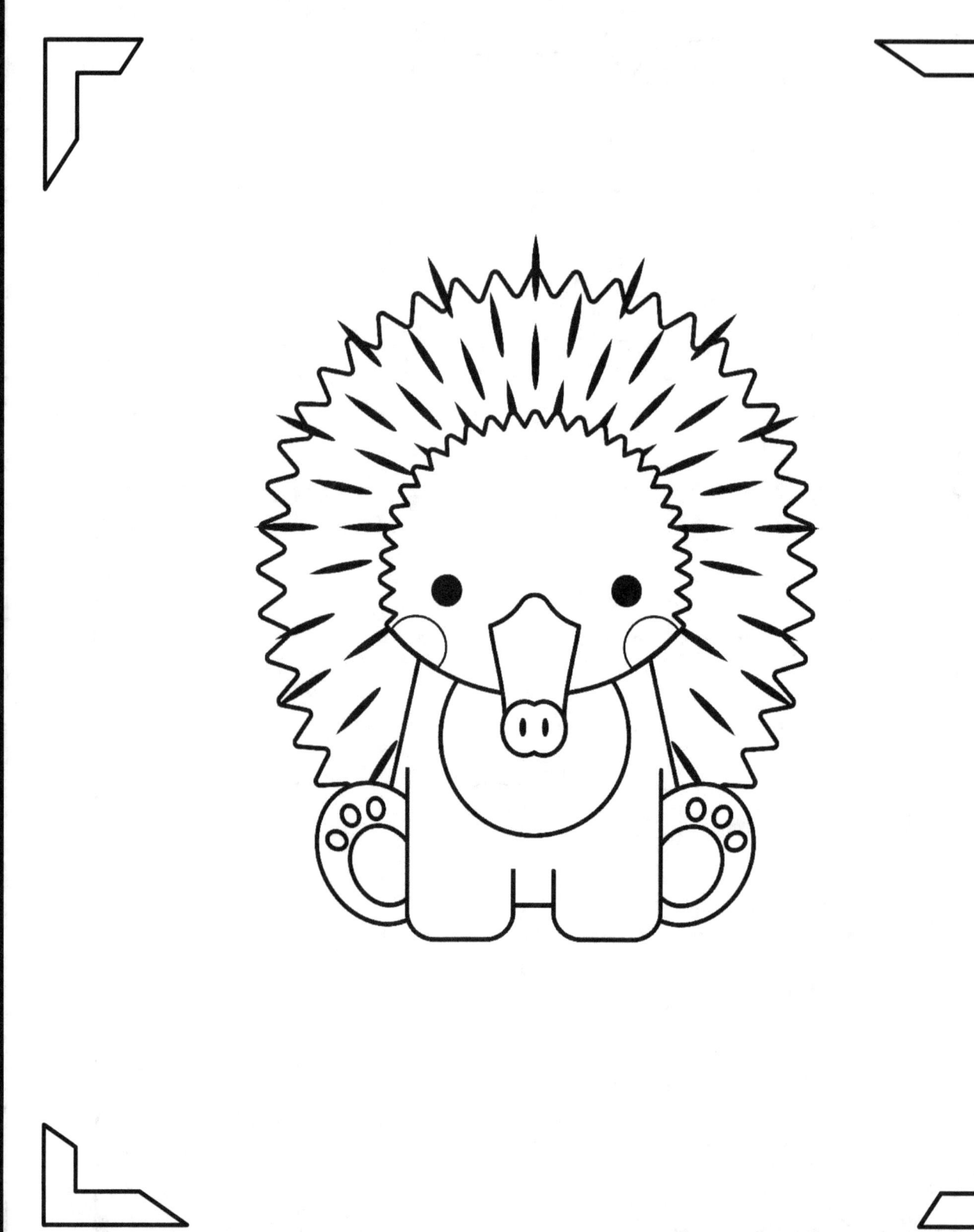

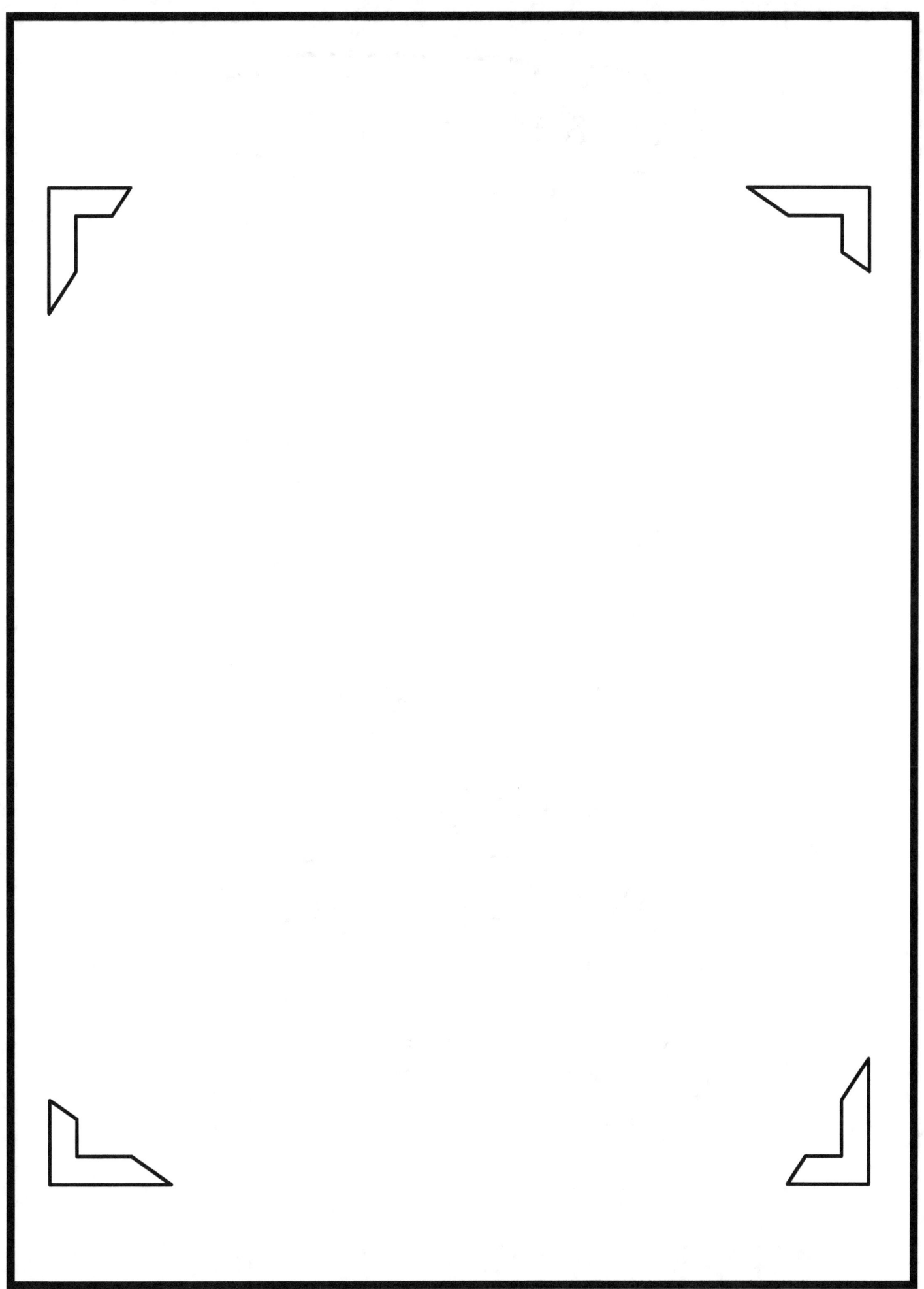

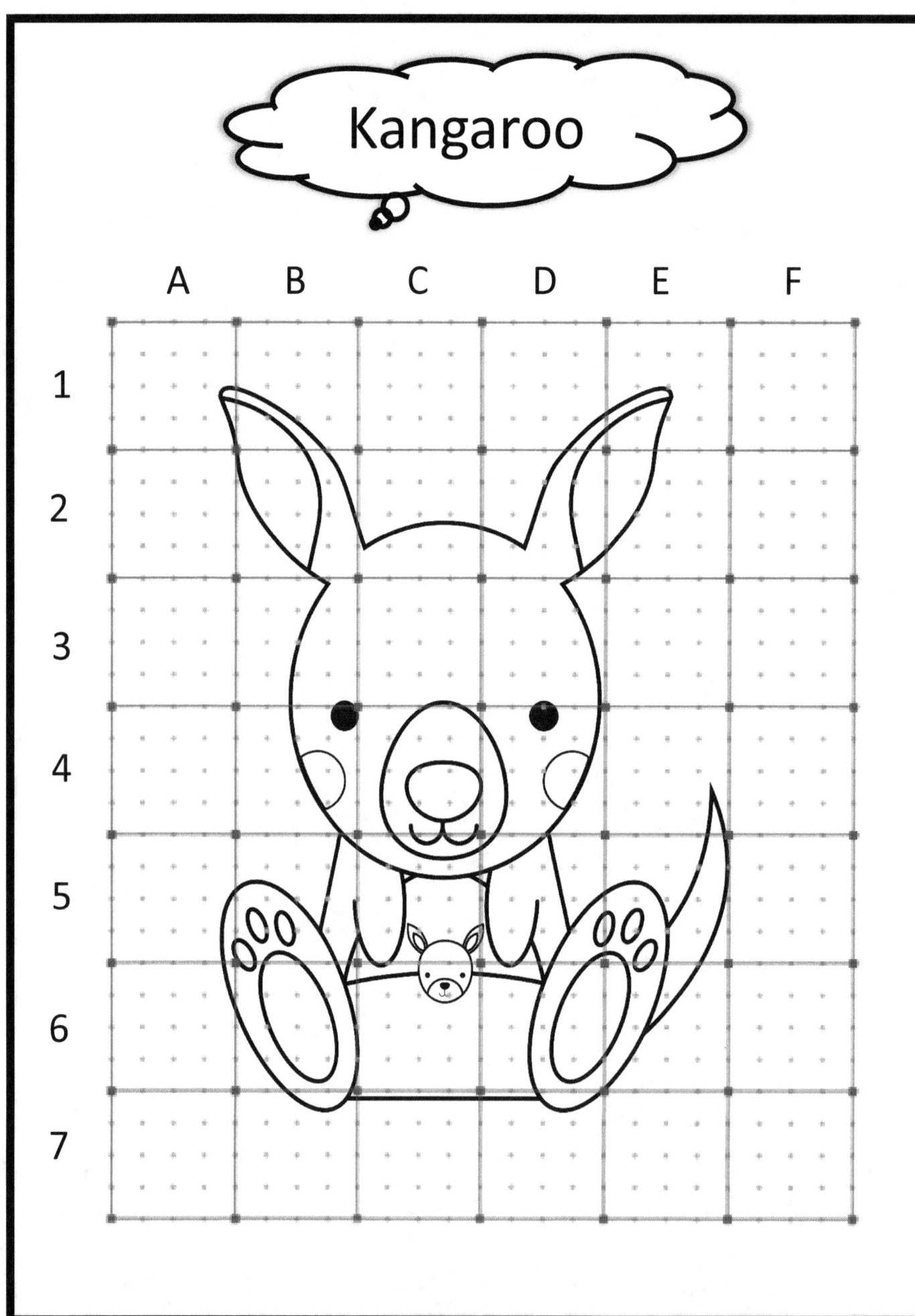

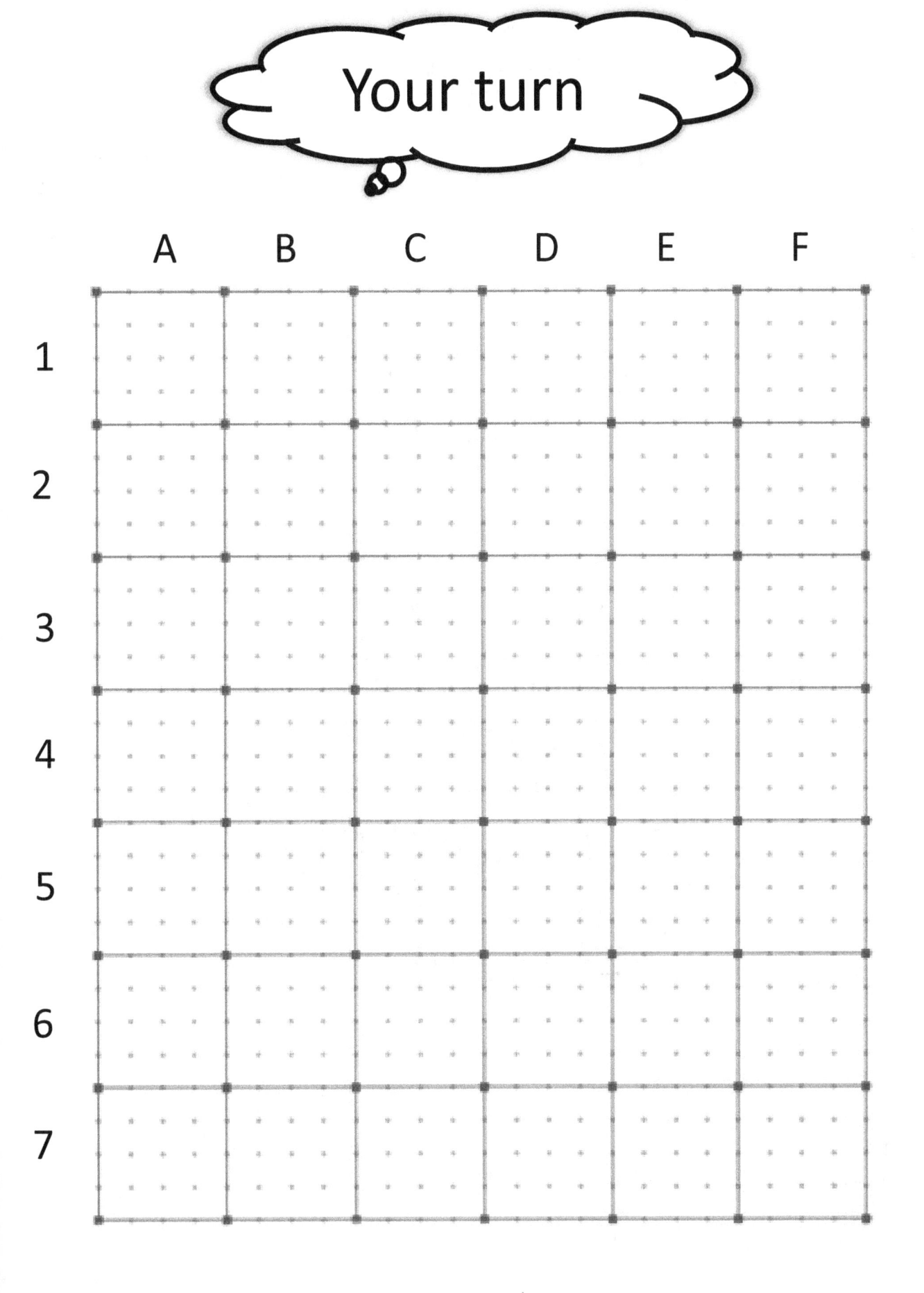

Trace It

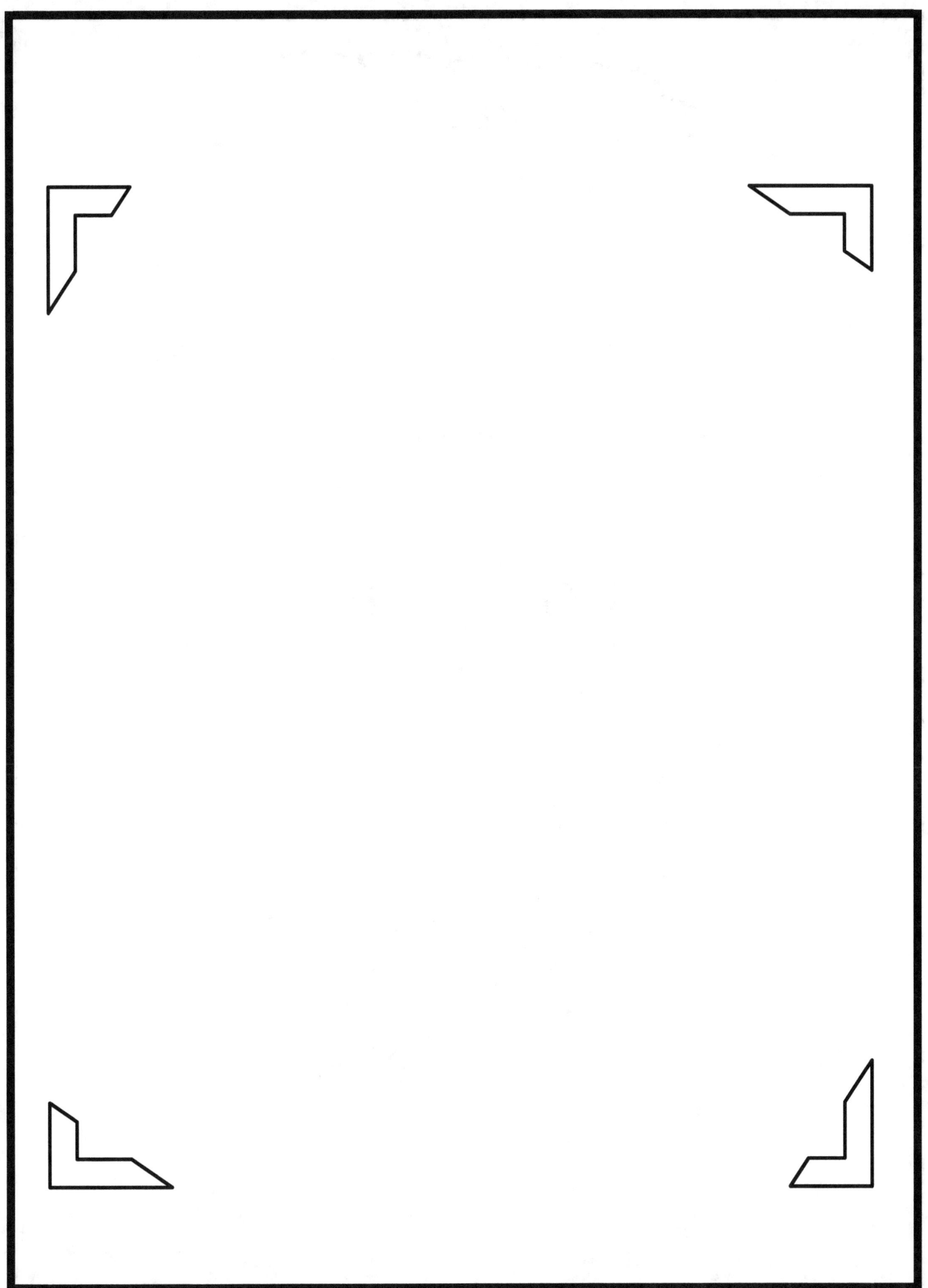

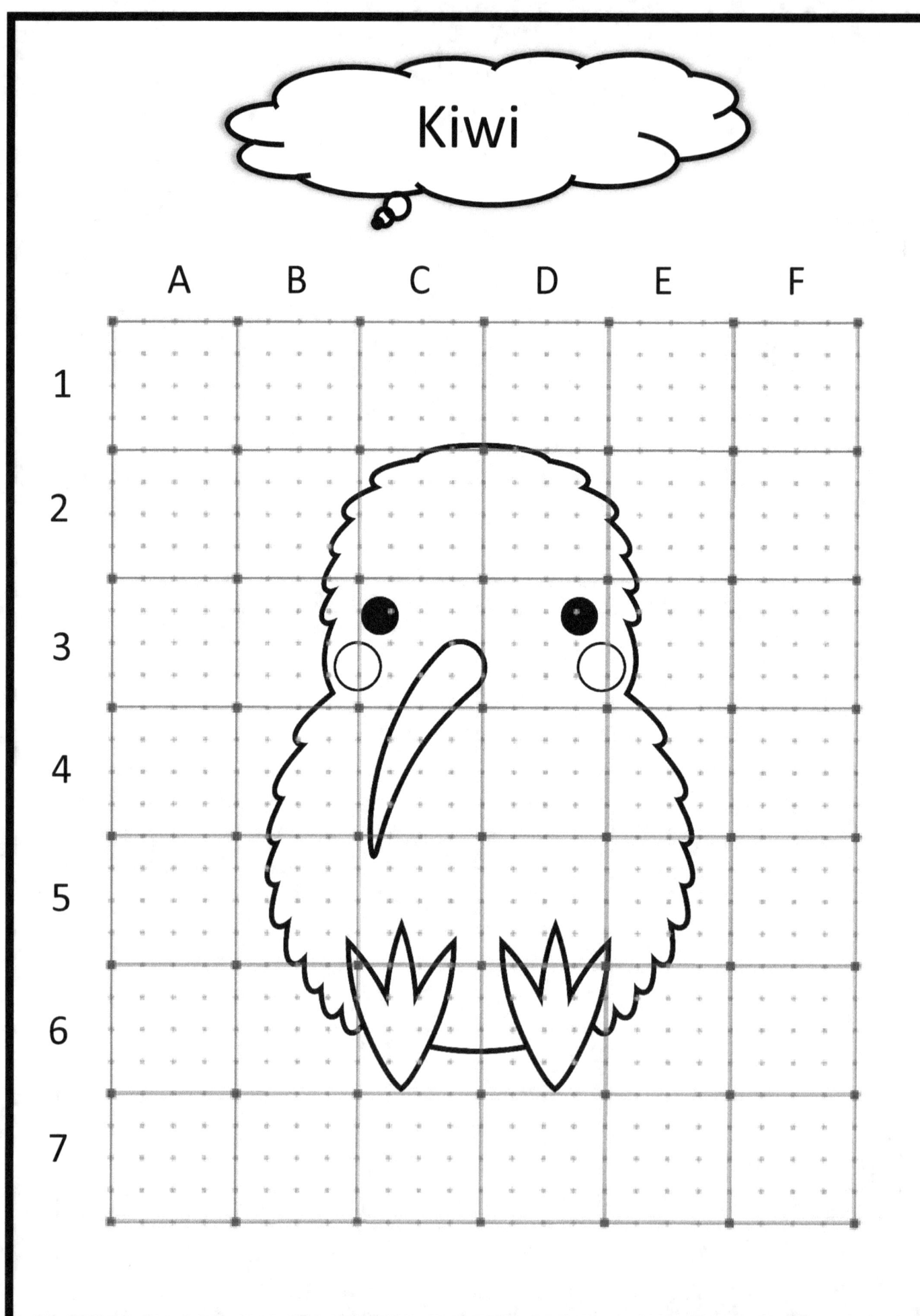

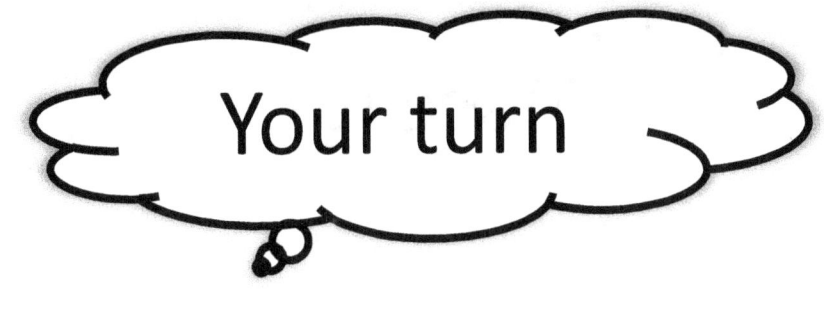

	A	B	C	D	E	F
1						
2						
3						
4						
5						
6						
7						

Trace It

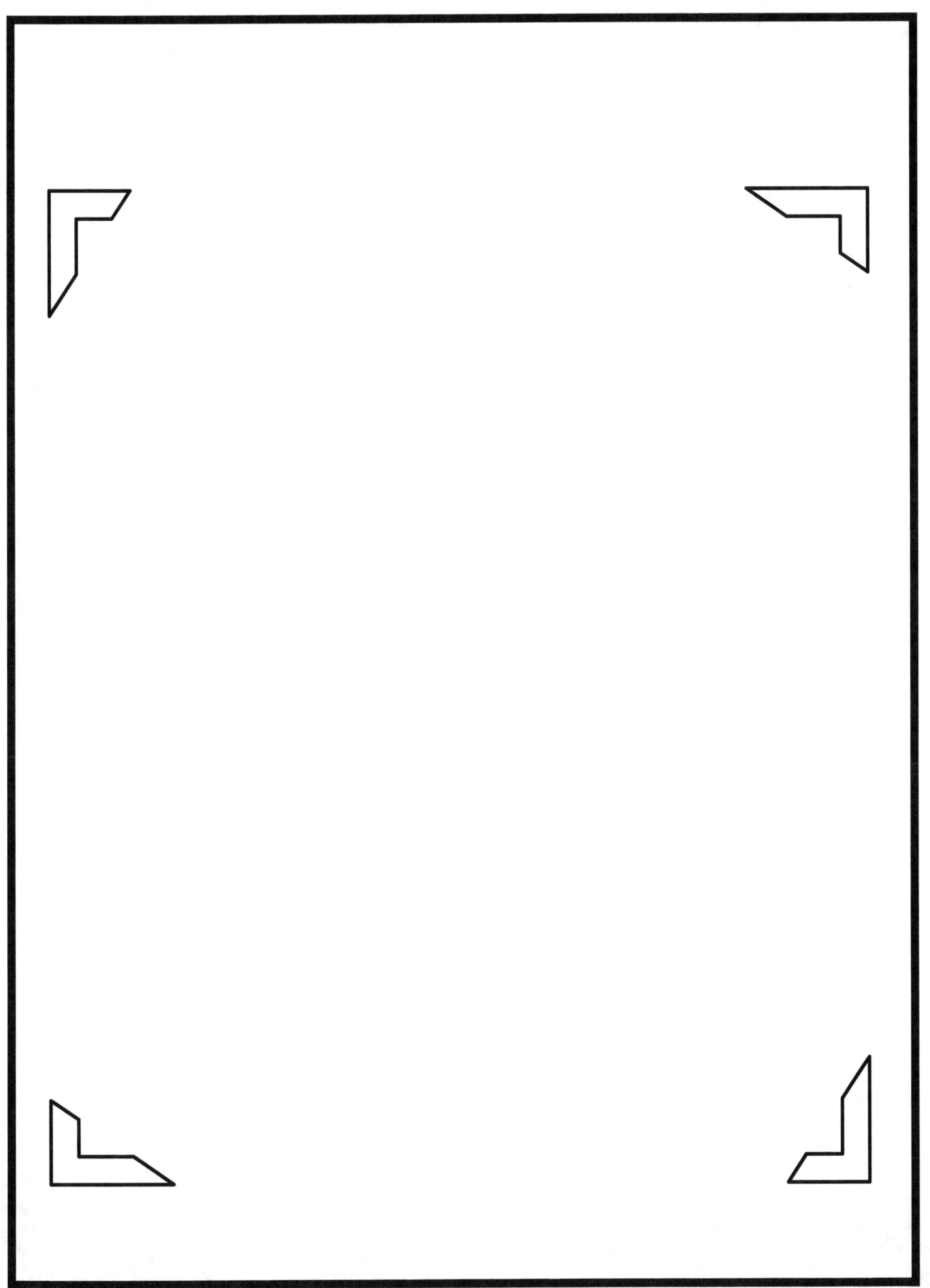

www.ingramcontent.com/pod-product-compliance
Lightning Source LLC
Chambersburg PA
CBHW060421220526
45465CB00008B/2970